A Treasury
of
Handmade Gifts

A Treasury
of
Handmade Gifts

Edited by Kate Yeates

CRESCENT BOOKS
NEW YORK · AVENEL, NEW JERSEY

First published in Great Britain in 1993 by
Anaya Publishers Ltd, London

This 1994 edition published by Crescent Books,
distributed by Outlet Book Company, Inc.,
a Random House Company, 40 Engelhard Avenue,
Avenel, New Jersey 07001

Random House
New York · Toronto · London · Sydney · Auckland

Copyright © Anaya Publishers Ltd 1993

With thanks to Hilary More, Pauline Butler
and Lindy Tristram for providing the
designs in this book.

ISBN 0-517-10342-7

Typeset by Servis Filmsetting Ltd, Manchester, UK
Printed and bound in Hong Kong

Contents

Introduction

The increasing popularity of craft shops and craft fairs is a clear sign that many of us love to give and to receive specially chosen and individually made presents.

A perfect present

What could be more exciting, and more rewarding, than making your own gifts for friends or family, each picked to match the recipient's character and taste? Most of these charming gift ideas are not only fun but quick to make and involve few tools and small quantities of materials.

Just for yourself

But the pretty things you make do not have to be reserved for others. Use up a leftover length of fabric or a roll of wallpaper to make yourself some of the delightfully decorative items shown here. Not only will they cost next to nothing but will provide your home with that cleverly coordinated look and personal touch that makes it look special.

This book sets out to inspire and successfully guide you through making over 80 decorative items for yourself and for others. In this book you will find:

● A photograph showing the finished result of each stunning article.

● A list of exactly what materials you need for each project, followed by clear step-by-step instructions that take you through from start to successful finish.

● Clear diagrams to match up with the instructions, help you to see how the item is made, and ensure a good result.

● Simple tips to help you avoid pitfalls and obtain a truly professional result. These furnish you with the simple information on modern techniques and provide you with the skills involved in traditional crafts.

● Simple projects taking only a minimum of time and money, leading on to the more complicated and beautiful items that you imagined only an expert could make. This allows those with only a little experience to gain confidence gradually.

● A source of inspiration for your own individual ideas. You can expand and develop some of the projects to give them your own personal touch.

Please note that many glues contain substances that can be dangerous if inhaled. Glue should be used in a well-ventilated room, and should be used by children ONLY under close adult supervision.

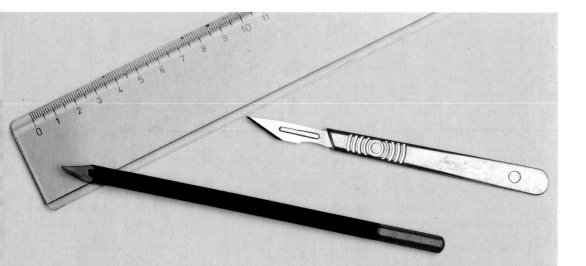

No-sew crafts

These sections involve no sewing whatsoever. Instead they cover ingenious ways of cutting, wrapping, covering and gluing paper, cardboard and fabric to provide a wide range of decorative items such as a smart desk set complete with covered books and files – ideal for the budding writer. We show you the easiest way to frame your loved ones' photographs or to give a mirror an attractive border. There are also unusual lampshades and wastepaper baskets; even cookie tins are given a lift with the addition of fabric.

Needlecrafts

These sections of the book are designed to build up from projects involving only the simplest stitchwork, so that even a novice can enjoy successful results. You'll then have the confidence to go on to the more complicated but highly decorative heirloom items.

The sections start with instructions for making perennial favorites such as sachets for sweet smelling potpourri and covered coat hangers, and go on to include curtain tie-backs and tablecloths for turning dark corners into interesting focal points. You'll find something to make, whether you only have a short time to spare, or several long evenings to extend your knowledge and skill.

Papercrafts

Here is a collection of papercrafts to appeal to all interests. Decorative papier-mâché bowls and beautiful jewelry, sophisticated decoupaged candlesticks, delicate paper lace pictures and origami are among the many imaginative projects.

Finally, the Better Techniques chapter gives more practical tips on how to ensure you make the perfect gift.

Involve the children in some of these projects. They will enjoy learning new skills and the next rainy day could be transformed into a delightful and rewarding time.

PART I

No-sew Crafts

Write minded

Give yourself the accessories in which to pen that bestseller – a matching desk set. Underneath is the blotter, made from colored posterboard, while the holders are covered in distinctive wrapping paper. Most work stations are somber places so why not treat yourself to a new desk set to encourage you to write that great work?

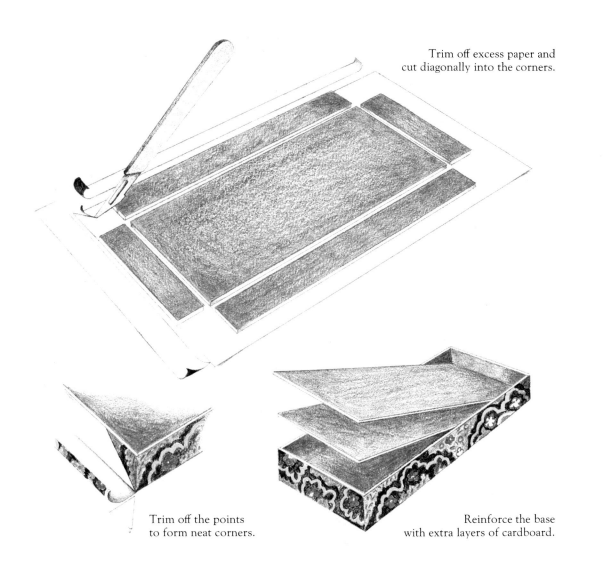

Trim off excess paper and cut diagonally into the corners.

Trim off the points to form neat corners.

Reinforce the base with extra layers of cardboard.

PENCIL TRAY

Materials
Thick colored cardboard or posterboard
   12 × 8in (30 × 20cm)
Wrapping paper 11 × 6in (28 × 15cm)
Paper cement
Craft scissors and sharp craft knife

To make pencil tray
1 From cardboard cut out a piece $7\frac{3}{4} \times 3$in (19.5 × 7.5cm) for base. Cut two long sides each $7\frac{3}{4} \times \frac{7}{8}$in (19.5 × 2cm) and two short sides each $3 \times \frac{7}{8}$in (7.5 × 2cm).

2 Lay the wrapping paper right side down. Apply paper cement on one side of cardboard base and stick centrally to paper. Repeat, to stick long sides on either side of base and then short sides. Leave a gap between each piece, the width of the cardboard thickness.

3 Trim along outer edges of side pieces, continuing at each corner until cut edges meet. Then cut diagonally into each corner up to corner of base.

4 Bring up the long sides, then the short sides. Trim and tuck edges of paper on long sides under paper on short sides; stick. Trim edges on short sides level with tray edge and stick in place.

5 To reinforce the base, cut two more pieces of cardboard slightly smaller than base and stick inside tray.

PEN/PENCIL HOLDER

Materials
Wrapping paper 17 × 14in (43 × 36cm)
Thick colored posterboard or cardboard
  15 × 9in (38 × 22.5cm)
Paper cement
Craft scissors and sharp craft knife

To make pen holder

1 Make up three sections. For the tallest section cut two pieces of board 2in (5cm) wide and two pieces of board 1⅝in (4cm) wide, by 5in (12.5cm) long. For the two smaller sections, cut card to the same width but 4in (10cm) and 1in (2.5cm) long.

2 Lay the wrapping paper right side down on a flat surface. Stick the board pieces side by side on the paper, with the space between each piece the thickness of the board. Trim paper to within 1in (2.5cm) of board on side edges. Trim paper level with top and base edges.

3 Roll up each holder and glue down, so the paper join is in the center of one side.

4 Glue the holders together, with seams hidden on the inside.

5 For base, cut out a 4¾in (12cm) square of board. Cut a square of paper the same size. Glue paper to one side of board, the underneath.

6 Glue holders centrally to uncovered side of base.

7 Cut strips of board to fit the spaces between holders and outer edge. Stick in place, to aid stability.

To make the tray and pen/pencil holder easy to clean, cover with a clear sticky-backed plastic, in the same way as with the paper.

Fix a square of blotting paper inside the tall pen/pencil holders, to catch any inky leaks.

Stick alternate widths of board side by side on the paper.

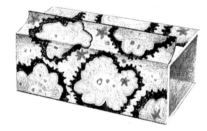

Position paper join centrally on one side of each holder.

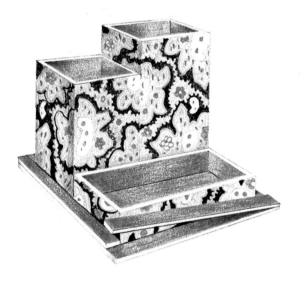

Add board strips between holders and outer edge.

BLOTTER

Materials

Thick colored posterboard or cardboard
  22in (56cm) square
Paper cement
Sharp craft knife
Blotting paper $20\frac{1}{4} \times 15\frac{1}{4}$in ($51 \times 39$cm)

To make blotter

1 Cut one piece of board 21×16in
(53×41cm). For corners cut two squares
4in (10cm). Cut each square in half
diagonally to form four triangles.

2 Make up each corner in the same way:
cut $\frac{3}{8}$in (1cm) wide strips of board and glue
to wrong side of each triangle along the two
straight edges. Trim off ends diagonally to
match corner pieces. Stick corner pieces in
place, by gluing down strip sections only,
making sure that outer edges match. Insert
blotting paper.

Trim ends diagonally
to match corner pieces.

Stick corners in place
only along added strips.

Under wraps

Give your favorite books a facelift with a new cover.

Nowadays with a huge range of wrapping paper on the market,

you will have unlimited choices.

Mix and match is the answer.

Materials

To cover two books: 6½in (16.5cm) square
   and 6 × 3½in (15 × 9cm)
Wrapping paper 14 × 7½in (35.5 × 19cm)
   and 8 × 7in (20 × 18cm)
Spray adhesive
Craft scissors and sharp craft knife

To cover the books

1 Cover each book in the same way. Lay
the wrapping paper right side down on a
flat surface, spray with adhesive.

2 Position open book with one edge to
within ½in (13mm) of one short side. Make
sure that the book is at right angles to the
paper edge. Close the book. Carefully
smooth the paper over the front cover.

Smooth paper over the book cover.

3 Run a fingernail down spine to crease the
paper, and continue sticking paper around
the back cover.

4 At the spine, open book and cut
overlapping paper into Vs. Push inside
spine.

5 Cut the overlapping paper across the
corners; fold remaining edges to inside and
stick in place, forming neat corners.

Push Vs up inside the spine.

You can cover any book in the same
way, just make sure you allow enough
give around the spine.

Glue the overlaps in place.

17

Box clever

Gone are the days when you kept bills in an old envelope in the kitchen drawer. Today you can choose colorful wrapping paper and make yourself a set of designer box files to display. Match the files to your office area or, because they look so good, sneak them into the bookcase.

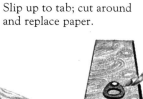

Slip up to tab; cut around
and replace paper.

Wrap paper around
back of box; spray to stick.

Materials

Box file, 14½ × 9½ × 3in (36.5 × 24 × 7.5cm)
  deep
Wrapping paper 32 × 16½in (81 × 42cm)
Spray adhesive
Craft scissors and sharp craft knife

To cover box file

1 Cut a piece of paper 22 × 16½in
(56 × 42cm). Reserve rest of paper.

2 Lay wrapping paper right side down on a
flat surface and spray with adhesive. Lay
box file centrally on paper with one short
edge butting against back hinge. Smooth
paper around body of file to opposite side.

3 Cut diagonally into paper at front
corners and fold in top and base edges.
Stick in place. Trim off excess paper at
front corners.

4 Turn in paper along front edge,
trimming paper, so it matches front edge.
Stick in place with edge to inside.

5 Using sharp craft knife cut around
button.

6 At back tab, cut into paper at right
angles to base, up to tab, and then cut out
circle to fit around tab. Stick and smooth
paper back in place.

7 For lid, cut a piece of paper 10 × 16in
(25 × 40.5cm). Spray with adhesive as
before, and stick to lid, butting left-hand
edge against back hinge and with an equal
amount of overlap at top and base edges.

8 Snip into front corners and stick overlap
to inside of box, trimming around the
catch.

Make sure that the paper is cut and
stuck on the box file with the design
running straight.

Make covered name tags for the spine
of the box: cut a piece of clear
adhesive-backed plastic 2½ × 1½in
(6.5 × 4cm). Write the contents on a
piece of card 2 × 1in (5 × 2.5cm). Place
card centrally behind plastic and stick
edges of plastic to spine of box file.

Alternatively cover each file with a
different wrapping paper.

Make sure that your craft knife is sharp
before trimming around the front
button and back tab.

19

Hat trick

Keep up with tradition and transform a plain hat
box into an elegant piece of luggage.
Even if you never wear a hat,
why not use this attractively-shaped box to store your love letters?

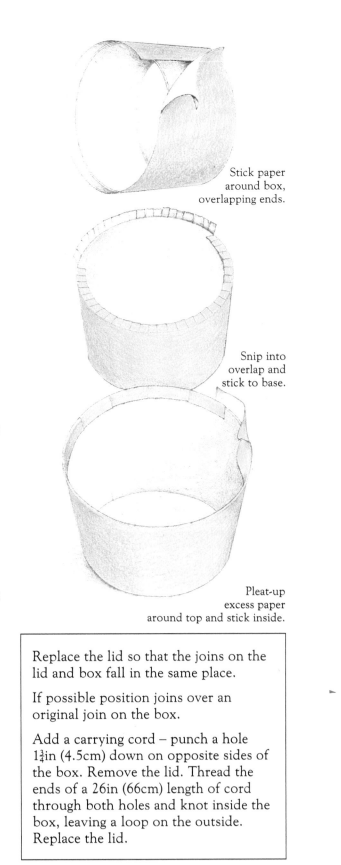

Materials

One hat box 6in (15cm) deep and 10½in (26.5cm) in diameter
Wrapping paper 34 × 22in (87 × 56cm)
Ruler
Spray adhesive
Craft scissors and sharp craft knife

To cover a hat box

1 Remove the lid and measure the circumference of the box, adding 1in (2.5cm) for join. Cut paper to this length by the depth of the box plus 1in (2.5cm).

2 Lay the paper right side down on a flat surface and spray with adhesive. Carefully lay the side of the box centrally on the paper at right angles to one end. Roll the paper around the box, smoothing out any air bubbles and creases. Overlap and stick down the ends. To achieve a good butt join, place a ruler over the join of double paper and carefully run a sharp craft knife down against the ruler. Peel away the excess paper.

3 At the base, snip into overlap of paper at ½in (13mm) intervals all around the box. Stick overlaps in place to base.

4 At top, turn overlap to the inside of the box and stick in place, forming small evenly-spaced tucks, if necessary, to pleat away excess paper.

5 For outside base, cut out a circle of paper, slightly smaller than diameter of box base. Stick to base covering raw edges.

6 For lid top, cut a circle of paper ¾in (2cm) larger than diameter of lid. Stick lid in the center of wrong side of paper. Snip into overlap at ½in (1.3cm) intervals all around. Stick overlap down onto sides.

7 To cover lid sides, measure circumference of lid and cut out one strip to this length plus 1in (2.5cm) for joins, by just under twice the lid depth.

8 Stick strip to lid side, over raw edges, placing top edge of strip to top edge of lid. Stick overlap to inside of lid.

Stick paper around box, overlapping ends.

Snip into overlap and stick to base.

Pleat-up excess paper around top and stick inside.

Replace the lid so that the joins on the lid and box fall in the same place.

If possible position joins over an original join on the box.

Add a carrying cord – punch a hole 1¾in (4.5cm) down on opposite sides of the box. Remove the lid. Thread the ends of a 26in (66cm) length of cord through both holes and knot inside the box, leaving a loop on the outside. Replace the lid.

Light work

Distinctive marbled paper in rich red and swirls of gold

transforms this plain shade into a leading light.

Add matching decorative braids to complete the ensemble.

This shade would look perfect in a study,

mixed and matched with a whole host of other rich furnishing hues.

Materials

Bought shade 8½in (21.5cm) high with 11½in
   (29cm) diameter base and 6in (15cm)
   diameter top
2 standard sheets of marbled wrapping
   paper
Wooden clothes pins
Brown paper for pattern
⅝yd (60cm) of ½in (13mm) wide decorative
   trimming
1⅛yd (1m) of 2in (5cm) wide decorative
   fringe trimming
Spray adhesives
Sharp craft knife
Fabric glue

To cover shade

1 Draw lines down the shade, to mark side
seam positions. Check each half is the same
size.

2 Pin the piece of brown paper over one
half of the shade. Using a pencil, mark the
outline of the shade on the paper. Remove
from shade and cut out.

3 Using the brown paper pattern, cut out
two pieces of marbled paper, adding a scant
½in (13mm) all around.

4 Spray adhesive on the wrong side of one
piece of paper. Line up the edge ½in (13mm)
over the marked side seam on lampshade
and stick in place.

5 Stick second half of shade in place
overlapping the first one at the sides.

6 To achieve a good butt join, run a craft
knife down the side seams, through both
layers of paper, remove excess paper.

7 Trim off top and base edges against top
and base edges of lampshade.

8 Cut decorative trimming to fit around
top edge and dip ends into fabric glue to
seal. Stick trimming round top edge,
slightly overlapping the top edge of shade
and placing seam over one of the paper
seams.

9 Cut fringe trim, seal ends, then stick
around base edge, slightly overlapping
shade.

Mark the shade outlines on the
wrong side of wrapping paper.

Match up the paper edges
to the side seams on basic shade.

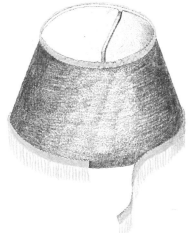

Add the base
fringe trimming
after sealing the ends.

Photo call

Frame the photos of your loved ones in a pretty print fabric. The basic shape is cut from cardboard and softly padded with cotton batting or polyfill. At the back a simple stand is anchored in place. You can make the frame to any size, with a square, rectangular or circular center to suit the shape of the photograph.

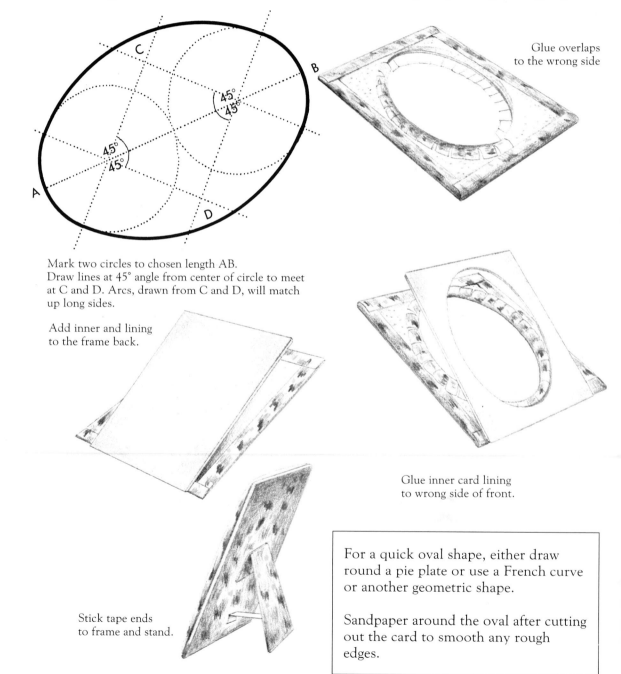

Glue overlaps
to the wrong side

Mark two circles to chosen length AB.
Draw lines at 45° angle from center of circle to meet
at C and D. Arcs, drawn from C and D, will match
up long sides.

Add inner and lining
to the frame back.

Glue inner card lining
to wrong side of front.

Stick tape ends
to frame and stand.

For a quick oval shape, either draw
round a pie plate or use a French curve
or another geometric shape.

Sandpaper around the oval after cutting
out the card to smooth any rough
edges.

28

Materials

Thick cardboard or posterboard 16 × 6in
  (40.5 × 15cm)
Thin cardboard 9 × 7in (23 × 18cm)
Printed cotton fabric 14 × 12in
  (35.5 × 30cm)
Lightweight cotton batting 6½ × 5in
  (16.5 × 12.5cm)
Fabric glue
Wooden clothes pins
4in (10cm) of ½in (13mm) wide tape
Scissors and craft knife

To make photo frame

1 From thick cardboard cut two pieces
each 6½ × 5in (16.5 × 12.5cm) for frame.

2 Make a pattern for an oval about 5 × 3¼in
(12.5 × 8cm) on spare paper, following the
diagram. Cut out pattern. Position to
center of frame front and draw around.
Cut out.

3 Stick batting to one side of front. Cut
out the center oval and discard.

4 Cut a piece of fabric 7½ × 6in (19 × 15cm).
Lay the fabric with right side down on a
flat surface; stick padded side of frame
front centrally to wrong side of fabric.
Bring raw edges to wrong side and stick in
place. Cut around the oval center, leaving
about ¾in (2cm) turning beyond the oval.
Snip into this fabric and glue to wrong side.

5 Cover the remaining piece of thick
cardboard with fabric for frame back; omit
wadding.

6 For backing pieces, cut two pieces of
thin cardboard 6¼ × 4½in (16 × 11.5cm).
Stick one piece centrally to inside of back,
matching base edges only. Place second
piece centrally to wrong side of front,
matching base edges only. Mark around
oval. Remove from frame and cut out oval
¼in (6mm) larger than frame oval and
discard. Stick backing to wrong side of
front, centrally with only base edges
matching.

7 To stick front frame to back, apply a
layer of glue around the frame edge,
making sure the backing cardboard is free
from glue. Press frame together and hold
with wooden clothes pins while drying.

8 For the stand, cut a piece of thick
cardboard 3¼ × 2½in (8 × 6cm). Mark the
center of stand lengthwise. Mark 1in
(2.5cm) on either side of center line. Join
up these marks to opposite corners. Cut
along these diagonal lines to shape the stand.

9 Cut a piece of fabric 12 × 3in
(30 × 7.5cm). Stick top of stand to within
¼in (6mm) of one end of fabric. Trim side
edges to ¼in (6mm) and turn in over stand
to opposite side and stick in place. Turn up
fabric over uncovered side of stand,
trimming and tucking under side edges in
line with cardboard edges; stick in place.

10 Trim off excess fabric on stand to
within 2in (5cm) of cardboard top. Fold
this flap of fabric in half and stick together.

11 Line up the base of the stand with the
frame and mark position of top of stand.
Glue flap of stand to back of frame at this
mark with stand above the flap. Leave to
dry. Bring the stand down over flap of fabric.

12 Turn under tape ends for ½in (13mm)
and stick ½in (13mm) up from base edge
with one end to stand and one end to back
of frame.

On reflection

*Take a simple mirror tile and turn it into a pretty hanging mirror
with cotton batting and print fabric.
Once covered, you can leave the frame plain or add decorative
cords, braids, sequins or bows, whatever takes your fancy.*

Materials
Thick cardboard 24 × 11in (61 × 28cm)
Cotton fabric 23 × 12in (58 × 30cm) 9in
  (23cm) square mirror tile
Cotton batting 10½in (26.5cm) square
12in (30cm) length of cord, for hanging
¾yd (70cm) length of decorative cord
Fabric glue
Compass
Darning needle
Wooden clothespins
Scissors and craft knife

To make framed mirror
1 From thick cardboard cut two pieces
each 10½in (26.5cm) square. Mark the
center of one piece, the front, by drawing
intersecting lines diagonally from corner to
corner. Using compass, mark an 8in (20cm)
circle centrally; cut out and discard.

2 Stick batting to one side of front. Cut
out central hole from batting and discard.

3 Cut an 11in (28cm) square of fabric and lay
right side down on a flat surface. Stick
batting side of cardboard centrally to fabric.
Bring raw edges to wrong side and stick in
place. Cut out central hole leaving ¾in (2cm)
margin for turning under. Snip into this
fabric and stick to wrong side of frame.

4 Peel off sticky pads on the back of the
mirror tile. Stick tile centrally to frame
back. Cut ½in (13mm) wide strips of
cardboard and, matching outer edges, stick
to edge of frame back, around the mirror
tile, until the sides are the same thickness
as the tile.

5 Make two holes for hanging cord on
either side of tile, ¾in (2cm) in from each
side edge and 4in (10cm) down from top edge.

6 Cut an 11in (28cm) square of fabric. Lay
the fabric right side down on a flat surface.
Stick back of mirror cardboard centrally to
fabric. Bring raw edges to mirror side of
cardboard and stick down. Trim off fabric
around mirror tile.

7 Turn cardboard over, feel for holes and
using sharp darning needle pierce fabric.
Thread cord through holes, so it is taut
across back. Knot ends on the inside; tuck
into the cardboard strips at each side and
stick in place.

8 Stick frame front over mirror back,
matching outer edges exactly. Hold with
wooden clothespins or place under heavy
books while the frame is drying.

9 Seal the ends of the decorative cord by
dipping them in fabric glue. Stick
decorative cord around the inner circle,
positioning seam in center of base of circle.

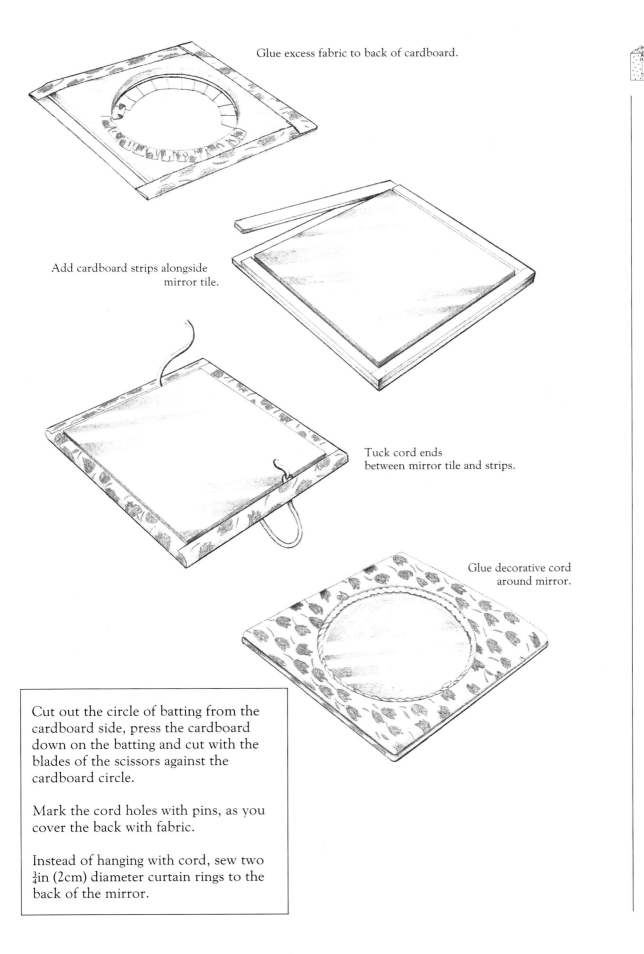

Glue excess fabric to back of cardboard.

Add cardboard strips alongside
mirror tile.

Tuck cord ends
between mirror tile and strips.

Glue decorative cord
around mirror.

Cut out the circle of batting from the
cardboard side, press the cardboard
down on the batting and cut with the
blades of the scissors against the
cardboard circle.

Mark the cord holes with pins, as you
cover the back with fabric.

Instead of hanging with cord, sew two
¾in (2cm) diameter curtain rings to the
back of the mirror.

Tissue transformation

Disguise a store-bought tissue box with a snazzy padded cover. The basic cover is made of cardboard, with layers of batting and fabric. Make one to match each bedroom, using remnants of upholstery fabric. Display with the cotton ball holder for a coordinated set.

Materials
Thick cardboard of 15 × 12in (38 × 30cm)
Lightweight batting 11 × 5in (28 × 12.5cm)
Upholstery fabric 22 × 14in (56 × 35.5cm)
Box of tissues
Fabric glue
Sharp craft knife and scissors

To make the tissue box cover
1 From cardboard cut one piece $10\frac{1}{4} \times 4\frac{3}{4}$in
(26 × 12cm) for top, two pieces each
$4\frac{3}{4} \times 2\frac{3}{4}$in (12 × 7cm) for short sides and two
pieces each $2\frac{3}{4} \times 10\frac{1}{4}$in (7 × 26cm) for long
sides.

2 Remove the oval from the box of tissues
and use as a template. Place centrally on
cardboard top and draw around. Using a
sharp craft knife carefully cut out oval and
discard.

3 Using cardboard as a template, cut a
piece of batting the same size as top, glue to
one side of cardboard top. Cut out oval
from wadding to match cardboard and
discard.

4 Cut a piece of fabric 1in (2.5cm) larger
all around than top section. Lay fabric right
side down on a flat surface, glue batted
section centrally on top. Bring raw fabric
edges over to wrong side and glue in place,
forming neat corners. Cut out center of
oval, leaving a border of about $\frac{3}{4}$in (2cm)
around oval. Snip into this border all
round at about $\frac{1}{2}$in (13mm) intervals and
stick to wrong side.

5 Cover the remaining pieces of cardboard
with fabric only. Place fabric pieces right
side down, glue cardboard centrally to
wrong side. Turn raw edges over to wrong
side and glue in place, forming neat
corners.

6 Place top section right side down on a
flat surface. Glue long sides to edge, then
the two short side pieces, slotting them in
between the long sections. Check that all
edges butt together before leaving to dry.

When cutting shaped areas from
cardboard run the craft knife carefully
around the shape to create a groove,
then go over the shape again, in the
groove, this time pressing hard enough
to cut the cardboard.
Add extra fabric glue inside the cover
to make the joins extra firm.

Cut out oval from batting
and discard.

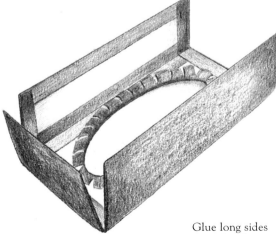

Glue overlap
to wrong side
of top around oval opening
and all outer edges.

Glue long sides
to wrong side of top,
then slot in short sides and glue.

Trinket box

Keep all your secrets locked away in this decoupage trinket box.

The domed lid is covered in flower heads,

while the inside is lined and softly padded.

We've kept the decoration unsealed to give a more raised effect.

Materials

Dome-shaped hinged wooden box,
  $5\frac{1}{2} \times 3\frac{1}{2} \times 3\frac{1}{4}$in (14 × 9 × 8cm) deep
Flat white spray paint
Sheet of floral wrapping paper
Clear glue
White felt 12 × 6in (30 × 15cm)
Plain cotton fabric 10 × 7in (25 × 17.5cm)
Lightweight batting the same size as fabric
Thin cardboard 7 × 6in (17.5 × 15cm)
Sharp board knife and scissors

To decorate trinket box

1 Spray paint the box, outside and inside.
Leave to dry.

2 Carefully cut flower heads from
wrapping paper. Arrange flower heads in
an oval ring on top of the lid and when the
arrangement looks good, glue in place.

3 Glue one flower head over the keyhole
in the front of the box. Cut out the
keyhole.

4 Measure the inside of the box and cut a
piece of white felt to fit each side. Glue felt
in place.

5 Measure inside the lid and cut a piece of
thin cardboard to this size. Using
cardboard as a template, cut one piece of
batting the same size. Cut a piece of fabric
1in (2.5cm) larger all around than the
cardboard.

6 Stick batting to one side of cardboard.
Place fabric right side down on a flat
surface. Glue batted side of cardboard
centrally to wrong side of fabric. Turn and
glue raw edges to wrong side of card. Glue
padded lid lining in place.

7 Repeat, to make a padded base for the
inside of the box in the same way.

8 Cut a piece of felt $5\frac{1}{2} \times 3\frac{1}{2}$in (14 × 9cm).
Glue to underside of box.

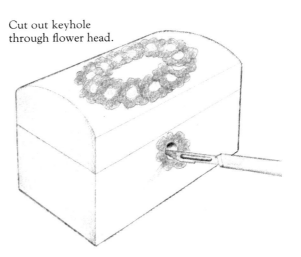

Cut out keyhole
through flower head.

Glue padded
lid lining in place
inside box.

Decorating the keyhole

Run an emery board over the painted
surface before gluing the flowers in
place, to provide a rough surface for
the adhesive. Decorate the key to
match the box. Cut a 5in (12.5cm)
length of ribbon and thread through
key end. Using a paper flower head as a
template, cut out two pieces of pink
felt the same shape. Glue the felt flower
heads together sandwiching ribbon
ends in between.

Floral arrangement

Design your own still life without drawing a line.
All you need to do is cut out lots of different flower shapes
to create a collage you'll be proud to hang on the wall.
Take the same idea to create a landscape picture of flowers
in a garden.

Materials

Backing cardboard 21 × 17½in (53 × 44.5cm)
Background fabric, the same size as
    cardboard
Spray adhesive
Remnant of floral fabric
Striped fabric for vase
Thin cardboard or posterboard 6in (15cm)
    square
Paper for pattern
Fabric glue
Sharp fabric scissors

To make the collage

1 Iron background fabric and using spray
adhesive, fix to backing cardboard,
matching outer edges.

2 Cut out flowers and leaves from floral
fabric.

3 Position flowers and leaves on
background fabric and arrange as a bunch.
Decide on the size and shape of the vase –
ours was about 5½ × 4in (14 × 10cm) – and
cut a piece of paper roughly to that size.
Fold in half lengthways. Draw one half of
vase shape freehand. Keeping the paper
folded, cut out the vase shape. Unfold.

4 Using paper pattern cut out a vase shape
from thin cardboard.

5 Cut out ⅝in (1.5cm) wide strips from
striped fabric and weave together over
cardboard vase; stick in place. Turn
cardboard over and trim off fabric to
match cardboard outline.

6 Stick vase centrally to background
fabric, 2in (5cm) up from base edge.

7 Rearrange flowers and leaves over
background fabric, around vase, until the
arrangement looks good, then carefully lift
each piece in turn and stick in place with
fabric glue. If necessary, mark positions of
motifs as you lift them with pins, so they
can be replaced in the exact position.

8 Leave to dry, then frame.

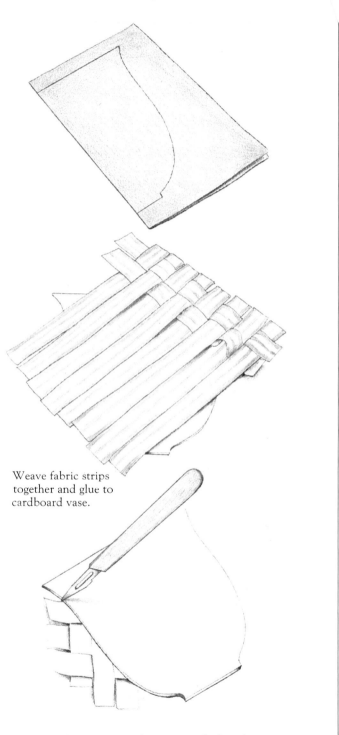

Draw vase freehand for the pattern.

Weave fabric strips
together and glue to
cardboard vase.

Turn cardboard over and trim around edge of vase.

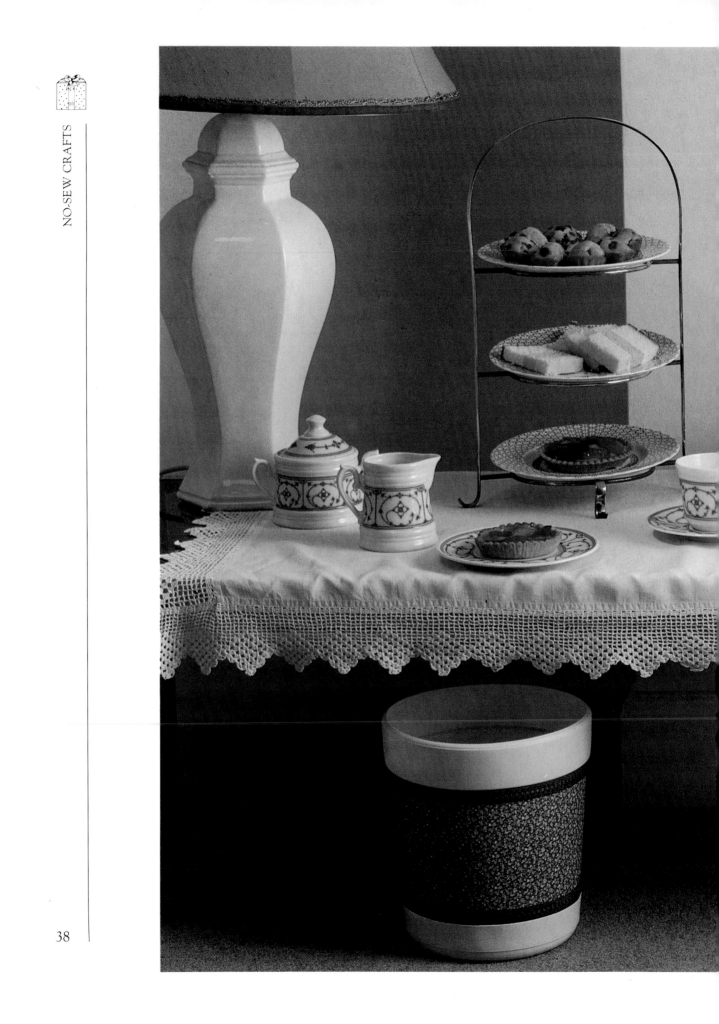

Waste not want not

Upgrade a boring metal or plastic wastepaper basket with pretty fabric and decorative cord.

You'll find it quick and easy to cover, whatever the size of the basic wasterpaper basket, so you can make one for every room where the waste paper threatens to take over.

Materials

Piece of upholstery fabric 40 × 25in
   (102 × 63cm)
1¼yd (1.5m) of decorative cord
Metal or plastic wastepaper basket, 10in
   (25.5cm) high
Spray and fabric glues
Wooden clothes pins
Braid (circumference of small
   tin + turn-under)

To cover the wastepaper basket

1 Measure the circumference at the widest part of the wastepaper basket. Cut a piece of fabric to this length plus 2in (5cm), by the depth of the basket plus 2in (5cm).

2 Temporarily hold the fabric to wastepaper basket with wooden clothespins and trim fabric to within 1in (2.5cm) of edges.

3 Spray the wrong side of fabric at one end with adhesive and place on the wastepaper basket at its seam. Cut along the fabric in a straight line, using the seam as a guide.

4 Continue spraying the fabric with adhesive and smoothing it around the wastepaper basket, eliminating any air bubbles or creases. Trim off the opposite edge straight, allowing a ¼in (6mm) overlap. Trim overlap and stick in place.

5 Trim off excess fabric at top and bottom just under rims of wastepaper basket.

6 Dip cut end of cord in fabric adhesive to seal. Stick cord around top edge of wastepaper basket, covering raw edge of fabric, and trim other end of cord so ends butt together. Dip remaining end in fabric glue to seal. Stick cord in place.

7 Repeat with cord at base edge of wastepaper basket.

8 Cover the center section only of the small wastepaper basket and trim with braid. Stick braid over raw edges of fabric in same way as cord.

Wastepaper baskets can be covered with wallpaper to match the room's décor in the same way.

Cut the fabric edge straight in line with seam on bin.

Trim off base edge, just above rim.

Seal ends and stick cord in place around top and base.

41

Cookie time

Brighten up the kitchen with a row of fabric covered cookie tins.

Use a fabric remnant leftover from the kitchen curtains

or just pick a printed fabric that fits in with the color scheme.

We domed the top with batting

and added a pretty braid around the lid.

Materials
Tin, 6in (15cm) high, 4½in (11.5cm) in
  diameter
Small amount of acrylic paint and brush
Fabric 15in (38cm) square
Lightweight batting 12 × 6in (30 × 15cm)
½yd (40cm) of ⅜in (1cm) wide braid
Spray and fabric glues

To cover cookie tin
1 Paint tin with acrylic paint to cover any
blemishes. Leave to dry.

2 Cut a circle of batting the same size as
lid, plus a circle of batting ¾in (2cm) smaller
than lid. With fabric glue, stick small circle
of batting centrally to lid, then cover with
larger circle of batting, to create a domed
effect. Leave to dry.

3 Cut a circle of fabric 1in (2.5cm) larger
than lid. Centrally place fabric right side up
over wadded lid. Pull fabric firmly over lid
and stick to the lid edge at opposite sides.
Repeat at right angles to first points.

4 Work around the lid sticking fabric at
opposite sides. Snip small Vs into overlap
to take away excess fabric, making sure
fabric is smooth. Trim off fabric above tin
rim.

5 Cut a length of braid to fit around lid.
Dip braid ends into fabric glue to seal the
ends. Stick braid around edge of lid,
butting edges together.

6 Put lid on tin. Measure around tin for
length of fabric, adding an extra 1in
(2.5cm). Measure from lid edge to base
adding an extra 1in (2.5cm). Cut a piece of
fabric to this size.

7 Spray fabric with adhesive and stick one
short edge to seam on tin. Continue
sticking fabric around tin, turning under
½in (13mm) at top and base edges. Turn
under opposite raw edge and stick over raw
edge at seam.

Dome the lid
with two layers of batting

Snip into fabric
to achieve a smooth fit.

Turn under all the
raw edges and stick to tin.

When you've covered your tin with
fabric, spray with a protective coating
to help keep the fabric clean.

Needlecrafts

Cushioned for comfort

*Add the final touch to a room with a collection of
decorative cushions, plain or ruffled. They'll
bring a sofa to life, take the hard edge off wooden or wicker chairs
and bring the pleasing addition of color to a neutral décor.*

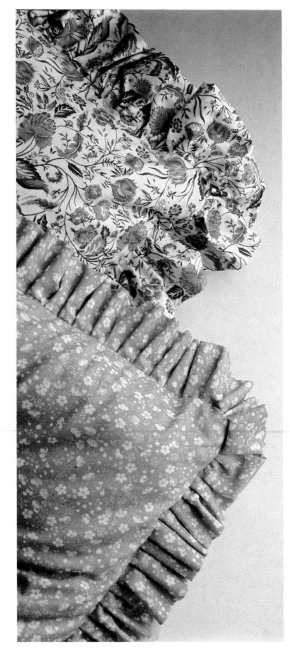

Materials
1yd (1m) of 36in (90cm) wide printed
   upholstery fabric
15in (38cm) square cushion pad
15in (38cm) zipper
Matching thread

To make a ruffled cushion
1 For cover front cut one piece of printed
fabric $16\frac{1}{4}$in (41cm) square. For cover back
cut one piece $16\frac{1}{4} \times 8\frac{3}{4}$in (41 × 22cm) for left-
hand section and one piece $16\frac{1}{4} \times 9$in
(41 × 23cm) for right-hand section.

2 For ruffle, cut out sufficient 6in (15cm)
wide bias strips, which, when stitched
together, will be twice the length of the
outer edge of cover front – 130in (330cm).

3 Turn under one edge of left-hand back
section for $\frac{5}{8}$in (1.5cm) and press; place
against the zipper teeth; baste and stitch,
using a zipper foot on the sewing machine.

4 Turn under one edge of right-hand back
section for 1in (2.5cm) and press. Overlap
this edge over zipper teeth and left-hand
edge for $\frac{1}{8}$in (3mm); baste and stitch, using
zipper foot on the sewing machine. Baste
across ends of zipper.

5 Pin and stitch the ruffle strips together to
form a ring, with plain flat seams, taking $\frac{5}{8}$in
(1.5cm) seam allowance. Trim and press
seams open. Fold ruffle in half lengthwise,
wrong sides together.

6 Divide ruffle into four equal sections and mark with pins. Work two rows of gathering stitches ⅝in (1.5cm) from raw edges in each section of ruffle, beginning and ending stitching at marking pins.

7 Mark the center of each cushion side with a pin.

8 Position ruffle on right side of cushion front, with ruffle facing inwards, gathering ⅝in (1.5cm) from outer edge and matching marking pins together. Pull up the gathering stitches evenly in each section in turn, allowing extra gathers at each corner. Pin gathers in place. Check that the gathers are even, then baste and stitch all around cover, ⅝in (1.5cm) from outer edge.

9 Open zipper. Place cover back to cover front with right sides together, enclosing ruffle, matching outer edges. Pin and stitch all around cover, following previous line of stitches.

10 Trim and zigzag stitch raw edges together. Turn cover to right side through zipper. Insert cushion pad and close zipper.

Before stitching cover front to back, pin ruffle edges to cushion front, so they will not get caught up in the stitching, when the cover pieces are joined together.

Add a double ruffle quickly and easily by inserting a length of pre-gathered cotton eyelet between the cushion front and main ruffle.

Turn under left-hand back edge and stitch against the zipper teeth.

Divide the folded ruffle into four equal lengths and gather each section.

Open zipper.
Stitch back to front over ruffle.

Circular tablecloths

*Hide a plain round table with a floor-length circular cloth
and turn it into the focal point of a room.
We kept the main cloth plain and made the top cloth out of lace
looped up at the sides with ribbon bows. Simply thread ribbon
through holes in the lace and tie in bows around the edge.*

Materials

Upholstery cotton fabric or lace, see below
  for amount
Matching thread
Paper, string and thumbtack for pattern
Scissors

To make the circular tablecloth

1 Measure the diameter of the table top
and the desired length. To calculate the
diameter of the cloth, add twice the table
height to the diameter of the table top, plus
½in (13mm) for hem.

2 Cut a sheet of paper slightly larger than
one quarter of the cloth. Cut a length of
string 10in (25.5cm) longer than half the
diameter of the cloth. Tie one end of the
string around the pointed end of a pencil.
Pin the other end of string to one corner of
the paper, with the string the exact length
of half of the cloth diameter. Draw an arc
from one side of the paper to the other,
keeping the string taut and holding the
thumbtack. Cut out the resulting pattern.

3 Fold the fabric in half and then in half
again in the opposite direction. Position the
paper with corners matching, cut out the
tablecloth. Unfold the fabric.

4 Turn under a double ¼in (6mm) wide
hem all around the outer edge of cloth. Pin,
baste and stitch hem in place.

To add ribbons: cut six 30in (76cm)
lengths of ¼in (6mm) wide ribbon.
Mark the outer edge of cloth into six
equal sections. Thread ribbon through
lace and over outer edge and tie into
bows.

If the fabric is not wide enough to cut
the cloth in one piece, seam two fabric
widths together with flat seams. Cut
one fabric width in half lengthwise and
seam to either side of one full-width
piece, so there will not be an unsightly
seam running across the table top.

Holding thumbtack
firmly in corner draw an arc
from side to side across the paper.

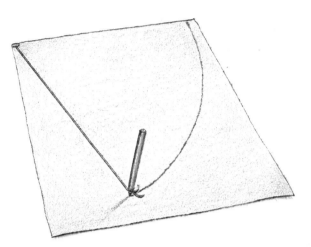

Cut out tablecloth
using the quarter paper pattern.

A touch of lace

Lower the lights and see the effect of a pretty lace lampshade.

Because of its romantic, timeless feel,

lace is always a favorite for soft furnishings.

Here it has been gathered and used to cover a plain lampshade,

so you can glimpse the design illuminated by the soft light.

Materials
Bought coolie lampshade, 8½in (21.5cm)
    high, 15in (38cm) diameter base and 4in
    (10cm) diameter top
1½yd (1.4m) of 12in (30cm) wide self-edged
    lace
Paper for pattern
Plain cotton fabric and thread
Spray fabric adhesive

Stick plain fabric
to basic shade.

Hand sew lace
around top edge of
shade.

To make lace-covered lampshade
1 Make up a pattern for the lampshade as
for the marbled shade (see page 25). Cut
out each piece from plain fabric. Spray
shade with adhesive and lay fabric pieces
on top, positioning two seams on either
side of shade at positions of light fixings.

2 Seam lace together with a narrow French
seam.

3 Work two rows of gathering stitches 2in
(5cm) down from top edge of lace. Pull up
stitches to fit top of shade, positioning
seam over one of the seams on shade. Sew
in place through gathering stitches.

Étui box

Based on a Chinese concept of a box within a box,

this étui is a small self-contained needlework box,

made up of fabric-covered cardboard leaves which,

when the lid is removed, open out to reveal all your sewing needs.

Étuis were first made by soldiers and seamen in the 19th century.

Materials
Printed cotton fabric 28½ × 11½in
   (72.5 × 29cm)
Plain fabric 10 × 8in (25 × 20cm)
Thick cardboard 18 × 11in (46 × 28cm)
Thin cardboard or poster board 10 × 6in
   (25.5 × 15cm)
½yd (50cm) of ½in (13mm) wide decorative
   braid
Lightweight batting 12 × 7½in (30 × 19cm)
1¼yd (1.1m) of ⅜in (1cm) wide ribbon
Fabric glue
Matching thread
Scissors and craft knife

To make étui

1 Cut out the cardboard pieces as follows:
From thick cardboard: four pieces **A**
4 × 3½in (10 × 9cm); one piece **D** 3½in (9cm)
square; four pieces **E** 3 × 1¾in (7.5 × 4.5cm);
one piece **H** 4 × 1in (10 × 2.5cm); two
pieces **J** 7¾ × ¾in (19.5 × 2cm) and one piece
K 3⅞in (9.8cm) square. From thin
cardboard: four pieces **B** 3¾ × 3¼in
(9.5 × 8cm); one piece **C** 3½in (9cm) square;
four pieces **F** 2¾ × 1½in (7 × 4cm); one piece
G 1¾in (4.5cm) square; four pieces **I** ⅞in
(2cm) square; and one piece **L** 3¾in (9.5cm)
square.

2 Using the cardboard pieces as templates
place them on the fabric. Cut out each
piece in turn, adding ½in (13mm) all around.

3 Using cardboard pieces as templates, cut
four pieces of batting the same size as
cardboard **B** and four pieces the same size
as cardboard **F**.

4 Lay each piece of fabric **A** right side
down on a flat surface. Position cardboard
A to fabric. Stick top and side edges to
wrong side of cardboard. Stick base edges
together to form flap.

5 Repeat, to cover pieces **B**, but glue a
layer of batting to the cardboard, before
covering with fabric. Stick all fabric edges
to wrong side.

6 Cut the ribbon into 4in (10cm) lengths.
Glue ½in (13mm) of ribbon centrally to the
back of each of the finished pieces **B**. Place
length of ribbon across the front and glue
remaining ½in (13mm) in place at the back.
Pull the ribbon tight when gluing.

7 Cover the back of the finished piece **B**
with glue except for ⅛in (3mm) around the
edge. Place this directly on top of the back
of finished piece **A**, leaving the base flap of
patterned fabric unglued, flat on the table.
Cover with a heavy book and allow to dry.

8 Cover cardboard **C** with fabric **C**, gluing all
four edges, turning neat corners. Leave to dry.

9 Place **C** wrong side up on a flat surface.
Lay **AB** padded side down and glue the
base flap of patterned fabric to the wrong
side of **C**, keeping the two pieces close
together. **AB** should butt up against the
square base **C**. Repeat on the remaining
three sides with remaining pieces, leave to dry.

10 Cover cardboard **D** with fabric **D** in the
same way as before, forming neat corners.
Leave to dry. Glue the whole of the wrong
side of **D** to within ⅛ (3mm) of the edge and
glue pieces **C** and **D** with wrong sides
together. Cover with a heavy book and
leave to dry.

11 Repeat, to make up pieces **E** in the
same way as for **A**. Repeat, to make up
pieces **F** in the same way as pieces **B**,
adding 2¼in (5.5cm) lengths of ribbon. Glue
E and **F** together in the same way as **A** and **B**.

12 Cover cardboard **G** with fabric **G**,
gluing all four sides. Glue four flaps of each
piece **EF** to wrong side of **G**. Leave to dry.
Glue the wrong side of **G** to within ⅛in
(3mm) of edge and place on top of **C**.

13 Fold under each end of fabric **H**. Place
cardboard side down on top of the fabric
and stick both long edges of fabric to the
cardboard to make the thimble box, wrong
side on inside.

14 Cover the four pieces of cardboard **I**
with fabric pieces **I**, gluing all four sides.
Slip these four pieces into the inner faces
of the box. Apply the glue carefully to the
base of box and press firmly in place until dry.

15 Lay each card **J** onto the fabric. Tuck
both short ends of the fabric in to exactly
match the card edges, applying glue to the

long cardboard edges and glue the fabric to the cardboard. Fold the length of cardboard into a square round cardboard piece **K**, wrong side out. Sew two edges together with small hemming stitches.

16 Make the top piece using the cardboard and fabric pieces **K**, gluing all four sides. Place the lid on top of the lid edge **J** and sew together with small hemming stitches.

Make the lid lining by covering cardbo᎐ **L** with fabric **L**, glue all four sides. A᎐ glue to the underside of the lid **K** and lining **L** into place.

17 Glue braid to the outer edge of to cover remaining raw edges. Tri᎐ seal braid so that the two raw edges butt᎐ together.

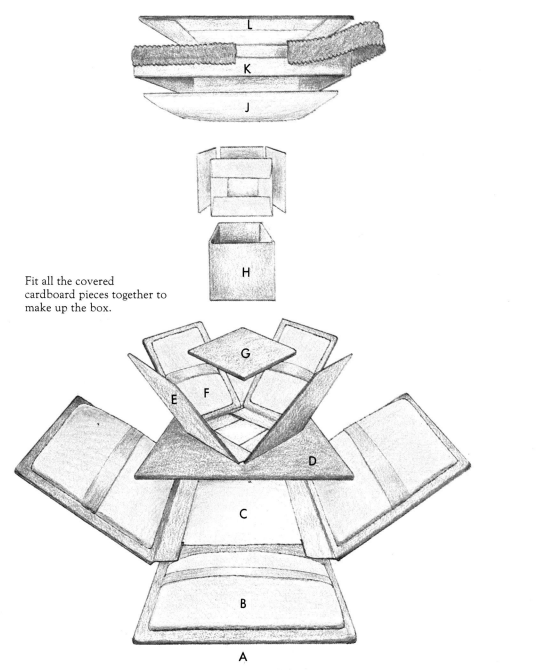

Fit all the covered cardboard pieces together to make up the box.

Make-up bag

*Keep your potions and lotions all zipped up in this little cosmetic
bag. The outer fabric is a pretty printed cotton,
while inside there is a practical wipe-clean lining.
Make one to match your bedroom, bathroom or handbag,
or choose a nursery print to take care of baby's needs.*

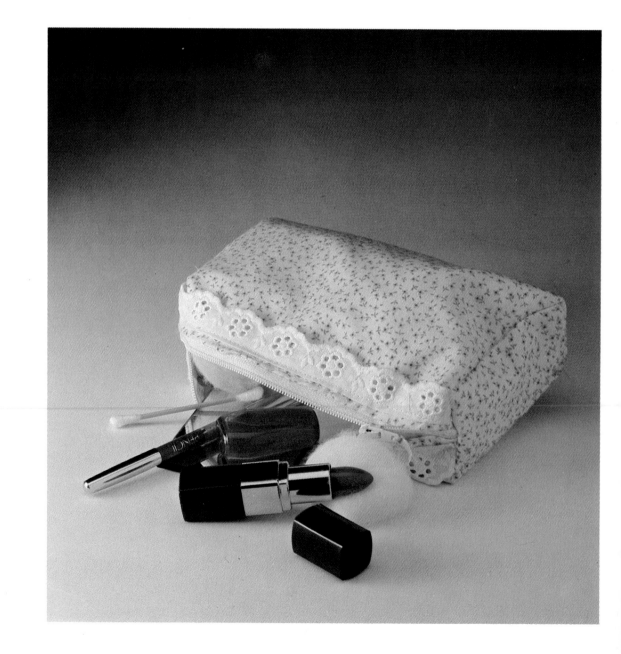

Materials
Printed cotton fabric 12in (30cm) square
Plastic lining the same size as fabric
8in (20cm) zipper
Small amount of ⅛in (3mm) wide ribbon
½yd (50cm) of 1in (2.5cm) wide cotton
    eyelet trim
Matching thread

To make make-up bag
1 From printed fabric cut one piece
12 × 9in (30 × 23cm). From plastic lining
cut one piece 11½ × 9in (29 × 23cm).

2 Lay the fabric piece right side down.
Position plastic lining centrally on top with
¼in (6mm) protruding at either end. Stitch
all around close to outer edges.

3 Fold fabric over plastic lining at each
side and baste. Place these edges on either
side of zipper. Pin, baste and stitch in place.

4 Place straight finished edge of cotton
eyelet along stitching lines on each side of
zipper. Pin and topstitch in place. Open
zipper.

5 From fabric and plastic lining cut two
side pieces each 5½ × 3in (14 × 7.5cm). On
one short edge, turn under ¼in (6mm) then
place plastic lining to fabric with wrong
sides together. Stitch all around close to
the outer edge.

6 With right sides together, pin sides to
main bag, with neatened edges across
zipper ends. Continue pinning down side
edges, snipping into corner diagonally to
help turn it neatly. Stitch all around,
pivoting stitching at base corners. Turn
right side out.

7 Cut a 2in (5cm) length of ribbon. Thread
through the zipper pull, knot and cut ends
diagonally.

You can make a 2in (5cm) tab of
double ribbon and insert it at the base
of zipper between zipper and side piece,
to hold when opening the zipper.

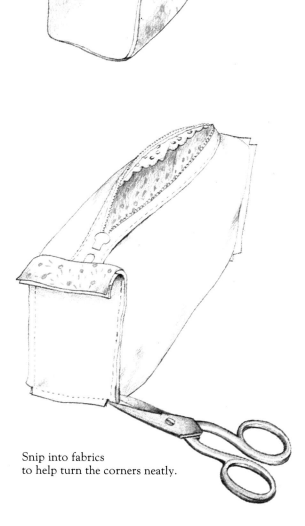

Stitch folded edges
on either side of zipper.

Snip into fabrics
to help turn the corners neatly.

Covered handsome hanger

Take a simple wooden coat hanger and turn it into
a stunning gift for a favorite friend.
You can also add a matching potpourri sachet to bring scent
and style to your closet.

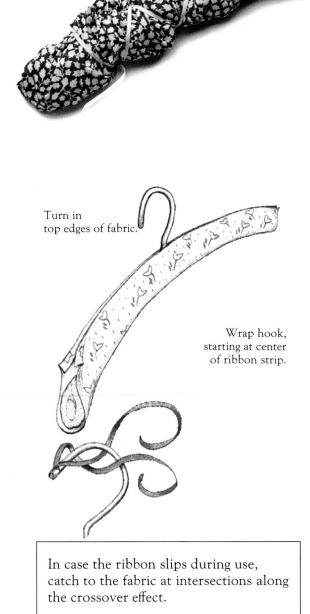

Turn in
top edges of fabric.

Wrap hook,
starting at center
of ribbon strip.

In case the ribbon slips during use,
catch to the fabric at intersections along
the crossover effect.

Materials
Wooden coat hanger
Fabric 32 × 8in (81 × 20cm)
Batting 18 × 4in (46 × 10cm)
Fabric glue
3½yd (3m) of ⅛in (3mm) wide satin ribbon
Small ribbon roses (optional)
Matching thread

To make covered coat hanger
1 Place the hanger centrally on the batting;
fold up batting around the hanger, stretch
it slightly to mold into the hanger shape.
Trim to fit and glue to the hanger.

2 Fold the fabric evenly in half around the
hanger, with wrong side inside. Turn top
edges to the inside for ½in (13mm) and pin,
so there is about ¼in (6mm) free above pins.

3 To gather top edge of fabric, stitch along
¼in (6mm) from folded edge through both
thicknesses using a large machine stitch,
and working from the hook to both side
edges.

4 Fasten both ends of thread around hook.
Pull up from outer edges and gather up
fabric evenly along the hanger. Fasten.

5 Fold ribbon in half and wrap center
point around hook end. Add a spot of glue
to hold ribbon end. Wrap ribbon
crisscross over hook and along hanger
working ends back towards the hook. Tie
ends in bow at base of hook and secure
with glue.

6 If desired, attach ribbon roses to the
ribbon intersections along top edge.

Cotton ball holder

Make up a handy drawstring bag to keep cotton balls together.
The cords are long enough to tie into a loop to hang over
a bathroom hook or the back of a door.
A boon when traveling, you can make up larger bags
for shoes, hairdryer or pantyhose and stockings.

Materials
Piece of printed fabric 17 × 6½in
 (43 × 16.5cm)
1⅜yd (1.3m) length of thin cord
Four toggles
Matching thread

To make cotton ball holder
1 Fold fabric in half widthwise with right
sides facing. Pin and stitch sides, taking ¼in
(6mm) seam allowance, to within 1in
(2.5cm) of top edge.

2 To form casing, turn down ½in (13mm) at
top edge and tuck under raw edge. Pin and
stitch along each casing. Tuck raw edges

Work a bar tack by hand at top of
each side seam.

inside casing at each end. Stitch a bar tack
at the top of side stitching.

3 Cut cord into two equal lengths. Thread
one piece of cord clockwise through casing,
thread on toggles and knot cord ends.

4 Thread second length of cord
anticlockwise through casing, thread on
toggles and knot cord ends, as before.

5 Pull up cords from each side to close
bag.

Potpourri sachet

Scent the whole room with sweet-smelling sachets.
Made in pretty print fabrics, these potpourri sachets
can be hung in closets and slipped into linen drawers.

Materials
Printed cotton fabrics in a variety of colors
Potpourri
Matching thread
$\frac{1}{8}$–$\frac{1}{4}$in (3–6mm) wide ribbon and $\frac{1}{2}$–$\frac{3}{4}$in (13–20mm) wide lace edging

To make potpourri sachets
1 The larger sachets: cut out 9in (23cm) diameter circles from fabric. The smaller sachets: cut out 6$\frac{1}{2}$in (16.5cm) circles.

2 Measure the circumference of each circle and cut a length of lace edging twice this measurement. Gather up the straight lace edge by hand.

3 Lay the fabric circle right side up, position the lace with gathered edge overlapping the outer edge of circle. Check that the gathers are even, then pin and zigzag stitch the lace in place, up to the join.

Pin gathered edging
all around fabric circle.

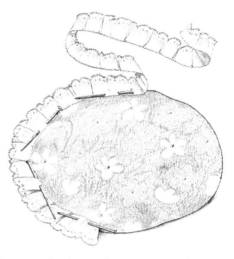

4 To join the lace edges, turn under raw edges, so they just overlap. Trim off excess lace, and continue stitching over the join.

5 Lay the fabric circle right side down; place a small amount of potpourri in the center. Gather up the fabric around the potpourri and hold in place by winding thread around the gathered-up fabric.

6 Loop ribbon around the sachet at thread and tie in a bow. Cut ends diagonally.

7 Alternatively, use two lengths of different colored ribbons to tie up the sachet.

Use small plates or saucers as templates to cut out the potpourri sachets. Simply place upside down on the wrong side of the fabric and draw around.

Jewelry roll

This neat little roll-up will slip into a suitcase to provide
a storage place for your jewelry when traveling on holiday.
There's room for all your rings, brooches and necklaces.
Make one to match the make-up bag
for a coordinated travel kit.

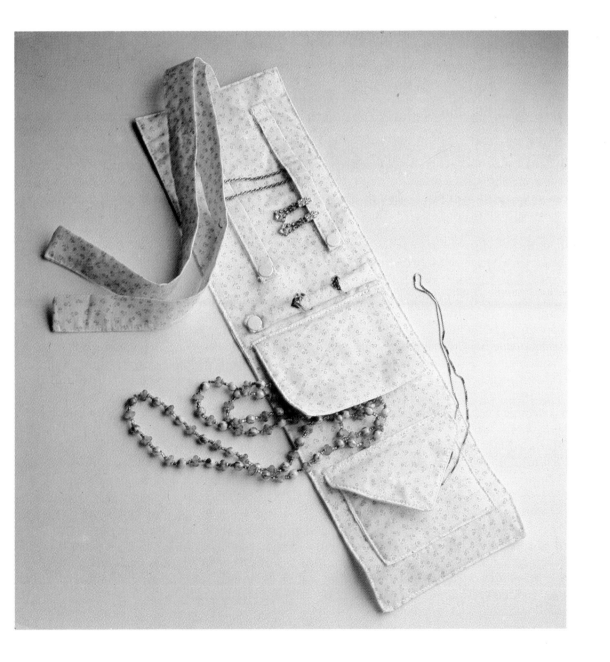

Materials
Printed fabric 36 × 17in (91 × 43cm)
Mediumweight iron-on interfacing
  19½ × 6½in (49.5 × 16.5cm)
Three white snaps
Six small snaps
Small amount of absorbent cotton wool
Scrap of lightweight batting
Matching thread

To make jewelry roll
1 For the main piece cut two pieces of fabric 19½ × 6½ (49.5 × 16.5cm). Fuse interfacing to wrong side of one fabric piece.

2 For the flap pocket cut a piece of fabric 7½ × 5in (19 × 12.5cm). Fold in half widthways; tuck under ½in (13mm) along raw edges. Cut a piece of batting to the size of folded fabric and place inside folded fabric; baste together all around. Topstitch across top edge.

3 Position pocket centrally 2in (5cm) up from one short edge on interfaced fabric; pin and topstitch in place close to outer edge on three sides.

4 Make a pocket flap, cut two pieces of fabric each 5½ × 4in (14 × 10cm). Place with wrong sides together. Stitch sides for 1in (2.5cm) then down to center in a V shape. Trim and turn right side out; press. Topstitch pointed edges. Turn in remaining straight edge for ½in (13mm); pin and baste. Position above pocket; topstitch in place across top straight edge.

5 Form pad by positioning a piece of batting 4½ × 3in (11 × 7.5cm) behind interfaced fabric 1½ (4cm) up from pocket. Pin and zigzag stitch in place.

6 Make a square flap over pad, by cutting two pieces of fabric each 5¾ × 4½in (14.5 × 11.5cm). Turn in ½in (13mm) around all edges. Place with wrong sides together, matching folded edges. Pin and topstitch one long and both short sides. Position over padded section and topstitch across remaining long edge to stitch it to background.

7 Make a ring holder by cutting a piece of fabric 6 × 1½in (15 × 4cm). Fold in half lengthwise; pin and stitch edges taking ¼in (6mm) seam allowance. Turn right side out. Fill with absorbent cotton, tuck under raw edges at each end and stitch to close. Position ½in (13mm) above padded section; stitch down one end. Fasten opposite end in place with snap.

8 Cut two pieces of fabric 12½ × 1¾in (31.5 × 4.5cm) for straps. Fold each strap in half lengthwise. Pin and stitch long edges, taking ¼in (6mm) seam allowance. Turn right side out. Turn in short edges, pin and topstitch all around strap.

9 Fold each strap in half and fix a white snap to fasten ends. Sew three small snaps along each strap, spaced ½in (13mm) apart, in from white snap.

10 Position the base half of each strap 1¼in (3cm) in from opposite side edge of background fabric, and 2in (5cm) apart. Pin and topstitch in place, leaving second half free, to fold over and fasten in place. Fix opposite halves of all snaps to background.

11 Cut a piece of fabric 32 × 2¼in (81 × 5.5cm) for fastening strap. Fold in half with right sides together. Pin and stitch raw edges together, taking ¼in (6mm) seam allowance and leaving a gap in the center for turning. Trim across corners and turn right side out. Turn in opening edges in line with remainder of the seam and slipstitch together to close. Topstitch around strap. Fold strap in half and position fold centrally at end of interfaced backing, fastening inwards.

12 Place interfaced backing with right side to plain backing. Pin, tack and stitch together all around, taking ½in (13mm) seam allowance and leaving a gap in the center in one side from turning. Trim across corners and turn right side out. Turn in open edges in line with remainder of the seam and slipstitch together to close. Topstitch all around roll.

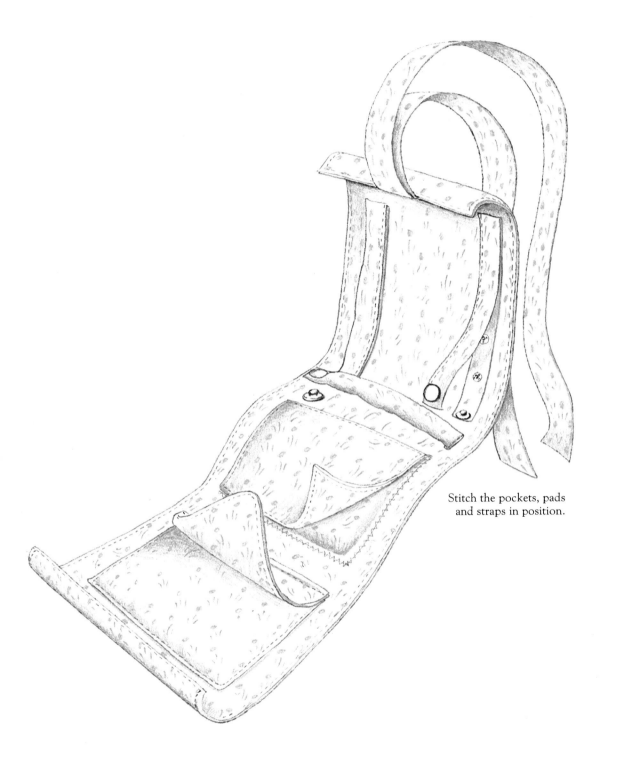

Stitch the pockets, pads
and straps in position.

Place mats

Lay a stylish table with bright gingham place mats.

They'll protect your table and give it a cheerful look.

There is a serving mat as well, for hot serving dishes.

Make both sides of the mat in the same fabric

or choose contrasting fabrics to double their use.

Materials

For two place mats and one serving mat:
¾yd (70cm) of 36in (90cm) wide gingham
Medium weight batting 32 × 22in
   (81 × 56cm)
4¼yd (4m) of 1in (2.5cm) wide bias binding
Matching threads

To make place mats

1 For one place mat, cut two pieces of fabric each 12½ × 9in (31.5 × 23cm) and one piece of batting the same size.

2 Place two fabric pieces with wrong sides together, sandwiching a piece of batting in between. Pin and baste together around the outer edges and at regular intervals across the fabric, to hold the three pieces firmly together.

3 Using a long stitch on the sewing machine, diagonally quilt across the fabric. Begin by working one row across the center from corner to corner, then work a line centrally across the mat in the opposite direction. Continue working quilting lines, on each side of first lines, 1½in (4cm) apart.

4 To round off the corners, place a small plate to one corner so sides of plate match fabric edges and mark around. Trim off corner. Use this corner as a template for trimming the remaining corners to match.

5 Press bias binding evenly in half. Place edge of mat inside folded bias binding. Begin centrally in one long side; pin, baste and topstitch binding in place. At end, tuck under raw edge of binding and overlap raw edge for ½in (13mm).

6 Make up second mat in the same way.

7 For serving mat, cut two pieces of fabric and two pieces of batting to 15½ × 12½in (39 × 31.5cm).

8 Make up serving mat in the same way, inserting two layers of batting in between the fabric pieces, and quilt across the mat in 3in (7.5cm) squares.

You can make up your binding from another fabric by simply cutting out bias strips and pressing them through a tape and binder maker.

Sandwich the batting between two fabric pieces; pin.

Use a plate as a template for rounding the corners.

Fold binding evenly in half around the outer edges.

Napkin rings

Avoid confusion at family meal times by making everyone a personalized napkin ring. We chose to make ours to match the gingham place mats, but you could make up a set of rings in different colors so that everyone will be able to recognize their own napkin. Add ribbon roses or ready-made embroidered initials to trim.

Materials for two rings:
Cylinder of cardboard from aluminum foil roll
Remnants of gingham fabric from place mats
Spray adhesive
⅞yd (90cm) of ⅜in (1cm) wide ribbon
Four small ribbon roses

To make napkin rings
1 Cut cylinder into two 1¼in (3cm) lengths.

2 Measure around cylinder and cut a piece of fabric to this measurement plus 1in (2.5cm) for overlap, by the length of the cylinder plus 1½in (4cm).

Glue the overlaps to the inside on both edges.

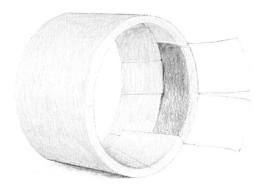

3 Place fabric right side down, spray with adhesive and place cylinder in the center. Smooth fabric around cylinder, overlapping edges. Trim overlap on one end to ½in (13mm). Snip overlap at sides at ½in (13mm) intervals; glue to inside of ring. Repeat with other side.

4 Make up second ring in the same way.

5 Cut ribbon in half. Tie each half into a bow. Glue bow and two ribbon roses over seam on each napkin ring. Cut ends of ribbon diagonally.

Check the size and thickness of the cardboard cylinders before you cut out your rings, as they do vary in size.

Curtain call

*Tie-backs add the finishing touch to curtains and
can be decorated with ruffles and trimmings to match the room:
plain, crisp-edged tie-backs with modern looks,
while ruffled tie-backs look best in chintz rooms.*

Materials
Upholstery cotton and heavyweight iron-
on interfacing, see below for amounts
Four ¾in (2cm) diameter curtain rings for
each pair of tie-backs
Paper for pattern
Lace edging (see below for amount)
Matching thread

To make tie-backs
1 Hold a tape measure around the pulled
back curtain to gauge the length of the tie
back. On a doubled sheet of paper draw a
rectangle to half this length by the chosen
width, matching one short edge to fold of
paper. Draw the shaped lines of the tie-
back freehand. Keeping the paper folded,
cut out the pattern. Check the size and
shape by pinning around the curtain.

2 Using pattern, cut out four tie-back
shapes from fabric, adding ⅝in (1.5cm) seam
allowance all around. Cut two pieces of
interfacing the same size as the pattern.

3 Fuse one piece of interfacing centrally to
wrong side of one fabric tie-back. Repeat
for second tie-back.

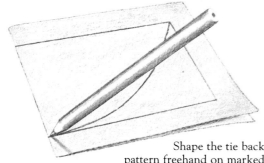

Shape the tie back
pattern freehand on marked
rectangle on folded paper.

4 Measure curved edge of tie-back and cut
lace edging for each tie-back to twice this
length. Turn under a narrow double hem at
each end of edging; pin and stitch. Gather
up top edge of edging to fit base edge of tie-
back. Position edging to right side of
interfaced tie-back, with gathering to
seamline and with lace facing inwards. Pin
and baste in place.

5 Match together interfaced tie-backs to
plain tie-backs with right sides together.
Pin, tack and stitch together all around,
leaving an opening in one side. Trim and
turn to right side. Turn in open edges in
line with remainder of seam, slipstitch
together.

6 Sew a curtain ring to the top point of
each tie-back.

Oven mitt

Bring food from the oven to table in safety with a practical oven mitt. Made from heavy cotton with layers of batting for insulation, the mitt is good to look at too.

We added a tape loop so you can hang your mitt near the oven.

Why not make two mitts so you'll be well covered in a hot situation?

Materials

Paper for pattern
Printed fabric 24 × 10in (61 × 25.5cm)
Plain cotton fabric the same size for lining
Medium weight batting 24 × 20in
   (61 × 51cm)
7in (18cm) of $\frac{1}{2}$in (13mm) wide tape
Matching thread

To make the oven mitt

1 Lay your hand on a sheet of paper with
the fingers spread apart. Draw freehand
around the hand in a rounded mitt shape.
Remove hand and cut out the pattern.
Check the size – the finished mitt should be
about 11in (28cm) long and about 8$\frac{1}{2}$in
(21.5cm) at the widest part.

2 Using pattern, cut two pieces from
printed fabric, two from plain fabric and
four pieces of batting, adding $\frac{1}{2}$in (13mm)
all round.

3 Pin and baste a piece of batting to wrong
side of each printed fabric mitt.

4 Place batting mitt pieces with right sides
together; pin, baste and stitch together all
around curved edge, leaving wrist edges
open. Turn under wrist edges and baste.
Turn right side out.

5 Pin and baste batting to plain mitt shapes
and seam together in the same way. Turn
under wrist edges and baste.

6 Slip plain fabric mitt inside printed
fabric mitt with batted sides together,
matching wrist edges together.

7 Fold tape into a 3in (7.5cm) loop. Fit
between the two layers at back of mitt. Pin,
tack and topstitch around wrist edges, with
two rows of stitching.

8 Make a couple of handstitches through
top of mitt to hold the print and plain
lining layers together.

You could cut the lining sections from
reflective curtain lining to help deflect
the heat.

Turn under
wrist edges; baste.

Slip plain mitt inside.

Fit loop between mitt sections;
topstitch around wrist.

Star bright

*Make a Victorian-style patchwork star in three different fabrics
to hang up as an ornament.
Change the fabrics to baby prints to make an alternative to a
mobile, or small Christmas fabrics for a festive decoration.
The points are finished with crystals and pearls.*

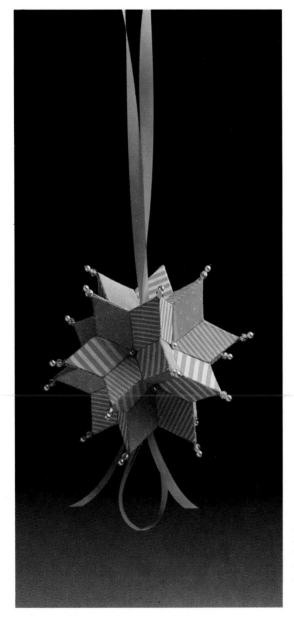

Materials
30 × 5in (76 × 12.5cm) each of three print
  fabrics
Card 15 × 8in (38 × 20cm)
1¼in (3cm) diamond patchwork template
Matching thread
Fabric glue
1¼yd (1.2m) of ⅜in (1cm) wide ribbon
20 pins
Ten matching pearl beads
20 pearl beads
20 crystal beads

To make the star
1 Using the template, cut out sixty
diamonds from cardboard.

2 Place fabric pieces wrong side up. Mark
around diamond template 20 times on each
fabric, allowing a ½in (13mm) margin all
around each one. Cut out the diamonds.

3 Place each fabric diamond right side
down and stick cardboard diamond
centrally to each piece. Carefully pull raw
edges over cardboard edge and stick to
wrong side.

4 Mixing the fabrics, stitch five diamonds
together to form a rosette. To sew the
diamonds together, place with right sides
together and work along one side with
hemming stitch. Open out. Hem third
diamond to second diamond and repeat,
until five diamonds are joined together.

5 Following the instructions in step 4 make another eleven rosettes of five diamonds. (You will now have twelve.)

6 Stitch a single pearl bead into center of ten rosettes.

7 Cut two 12in (30cm) lengths of ribbon. Match together. Fold in half to form loops, push ends through center of one plain rosette and fasten on the wrong side. This will be the base rosette.

8 Form a loop with the remaining ribbon, push through center of last plain rosette and fasten on wrong side. This will be the top rosette.

9 Take the base rosette and sew a rosette to each pair of sides. Then sew the rosettes together around the side edges. Repeat, to make up the top rosette in the same way. Note: you will now have to sew from the outside.

11 Sew the top and base halves together, along the remaining free edges, again using small hemming stitches.

12 Thread a pearl bead and then crystal bead onto each pin and pin into each of the twenty points in turn on the star.

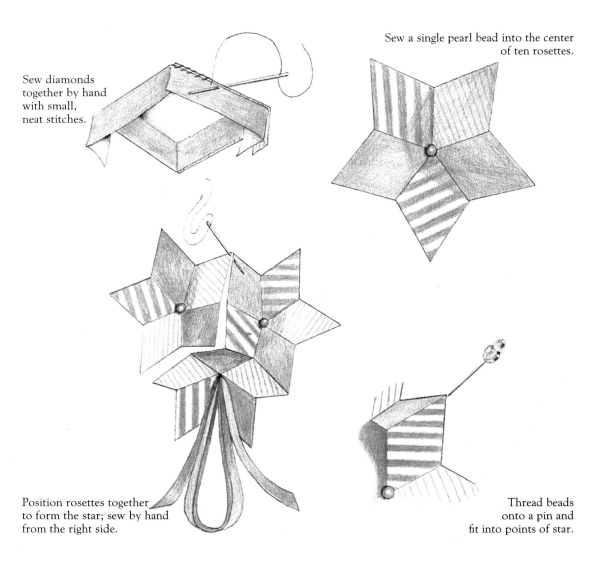

Sew diamonds together by hand with small, neat stitches.

Sew a single pearl bead into the center of ten rosettes.

Position rosettes together to form the star; sew by hand from the right side.

Thread beads onto a pin and fit into points of star.

Baby quilt

The perfect gift for the mother-to-be or for a newborn baby.
The patchwork design is called Baby Blocks, made up
of three diamonds arranged to look like a child's building block.
The completed patchwork is hand quilted to give
a raised relief effect to the whole design.

Materials

40 × 10in (102 × 25cm) piece of cotton
   fabric in each of three different designs,
   plus extra for border strips
2½in (6cm) diamond template
Paper for backing patchwork shapes
Mediumweight batting and piece of plain
   cotton for backing each 30 × 37in
   (76 × 94cm)
Buttonhole thread, for quilting
Matching thread

To make the patchwork quilt

1 Using the patchwork template cut out a
paper shape for each of the 93 diamonds.

2 Using template mark out diamonds on
the wrong side of each fabric, allowing an
extra ¼in (6mm) all around each piece. Cut
out each shape.

3 Position a paper shape centrally to
wrong side of fabric shape, pin in position.

4 Turn the seam allowance over the paper
backing on each side of the diamond in
turn; baste in place through paper shape.

5 To form each block, position a set of
three diamonds as shown, with one
diamond turned sideways over two more
diamonds. Make up as many blocks as you
need for the quilt – this quilt has seven
rows of 4½ blocks.

6 To sew the blocks together, place two diamonds with right sides together and oversew the matched edges together exactly.

7 Once you have made up your blocks, stitch them together into the size of the quilt center. As the patchwork center has straight edges it will be necessary to have half blocks, in alternate rows.

8 Once the patchwork is finished, measure the length and cut two pieces each 3¾in (9.5cm) wide for border strips. Pin, baste and stitch strips first to side edges, taking ¼in (6mm) seam allowance on patchwork and ½in (13mm) seam on border strip. Trim and press flat. Then pin and stitch border strips to top and lower edges in the same way. Trim and press flat.

9 Add a second border in the same way.

10 Cut a piece of batting to size of quilt and pin and baste to wrong side, around outer edges and across quilt at regular intervals.

11 Using buttonhole thread, quilt by hand, taking small running stitches around the patchwork shapes and to form a diagonal design along the border sections.

12 After quilting, place the patchwork with right side to backing fabric; pin and stitch together all around, leaving an opening in lower edge, for turning. Trim and turn quilt to the right side. Turn in opening edges in line with the remainder of the seam and slipstitch together to close.

13 Anchor backing to quilted front by quilting around the quilt in between patchwork and the first and second border strips.

Turn seam allowance over paper shape and baste all around.

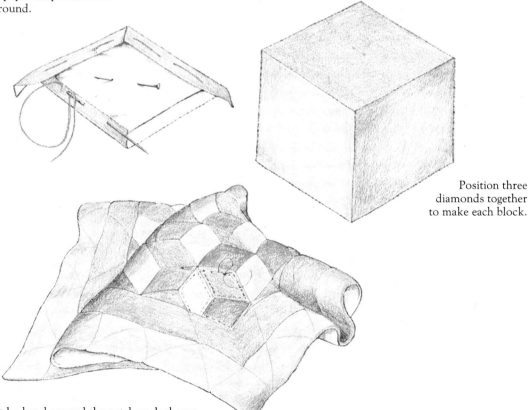

Position three diamonds together to make each block.

Quilt by hand around the patchwork shapes, using buttonhole thread.

PART II
More No-sew Crafts

Flower time

Fantasy time – a flower which can also tell the time. Cut from a cork tile and covered with felt petals this clock has ladybug numbers and filigree hands.

Materials
Cork tile, 12in (30cm) square
Yellow felt, 12in (30cm) square
Small scraps of orange and red felts
Pair of clock hands and movement
Few red and black beads
4 ladybug buttons
Craftweight interfacing, 12in (30cm) square
Fabric glue
Sharp craft knife

Preparation
1 Draw the pattern for the flower from the graph pattern (scale 1 sq = 1in (2.5cm)). Cut out the pattern and trace down onto the back of the cork tile. Carefully cut out the flower shape.

2 From the pattern trace off each petal, making each one slightly larger along the side edges. Cut 5 petals from yellow felt.

Making the clock
3 Stick a circle of interfacing over the right side of the cork tile flower shape. Turn the tile over and trim the interfacing along the edges of the cork flower.

4 Stick the felt petals in place, overlapping them.

5 Using the paper pattern, cut the larger central circle from orange felt using pinking shears. Cut the smaller circle from red felt, again using pinking shears. Stick the circles in place, one on top of the other.

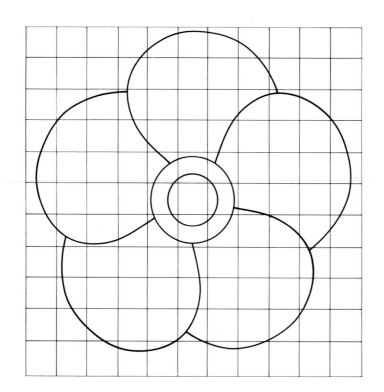

Scale 1 sq = 1in (2.5cm)

6 Drill through the center of the flower shape and fix the hands in place, with the clock movement on the wrong side, following the manufacturers' instructions.

7 Stick beads along the edges of the petals and in between, alternating red and black (see picture).

8 Make an indentation at the 12, 6, 9 and 3 o'clock positions using a knife tip. Stick 4 ladybug buttons in place.

Glue the overlapping felt petals to the interfacing side of the cork tile

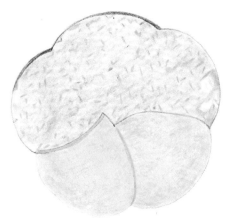

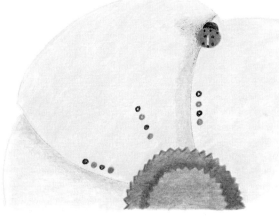

Glue the ladybug buttons in place at 12, 3, 6 and 9.

Clever candlesticks

Flour, salt and water mixed together make a pliable dough which you can use to model these pretty candle holders.

Materials
4oz (100g) of all-purpose flour
3oz (75g) of salt
Hot water
10 cloves
Watercolor or acrylic paints; brush
Spray varnish

Preparation
1 Dissolve the salt in a little hot water. Add cold water. Mix into the flour to make a moist dough. (Add more water if necessary.) Knead the dough well until it is smooth and elastic. Place on a lightly floured board.

Making the apple candlestick
2 Roll out a small amount of dough and, using a cutter (or a cup or mug as a template) cut out a circle, large enough to fit a 2in (5cm)-diameter candle plus an edge. Place the circle of dough on a baking sheet. Hand-roll 2 pieces into thin 'sausages', long enough to fit around the

circumference of the circle. Twist them together. Fix the twisted strips around the circle with a little water, trimming the ends so that they fit together.

3 Roll 10 dough balls the size of marbles for apples. Fit a clove into one end for the stalk. Roll out more dough and cut out 15 tiny leaves. Moisten the leaves and apples and arrange the apples in evenly-spaced pairs, around the twisted edge, each with 3 leaves.

4 Bake the dough model in a cool oven – 225°F (gas mark ¼), until baked hard. Remove from the oven and leave for a few days to dry out completely.

Cut leaves from rolled dough using a sharp knife

Twist strips of dough together to fit around the base

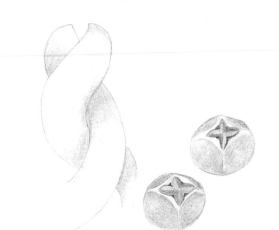

5 Paint the apples red and the leaves green. Leave to dry. When dry, spray varnish all over the candlestick.

Flower candlestick
6 Make up more salt dough in the same way as for the apple candlestick. Roll out the dough, cut petals and make up 10 roses.

Push cloves into the dough balls for apples

7 Form a base in the same way as before. Cut out leaves, moisten with water and fix them, overlapping, all around the base. Arrange the roses.

8 Bake the dough candlestick as before. Paint the leaves green and roses mauve and pink. Leave to dry. Spray with varnish.

Dancing feet

Give a plain pair of canvas shoes a party look with some individual decorations. Whether you prefer beads or shells your shoes will be unique.

Materials
Pair of plain-colored canvas shoes
Selection of shells
Glue
42 medium-sized turquoise beads, 46 small
   white beads
2 green, 2 white plastic leaves
4 pink plastic trumpet flowers
Matching threads
Fabric glue or Superglue

Preparation

1 Fill the toe end of the shoes with tissue paper to hold the shape while you add the decorations.

2 Shell shoes: Carefully glue each shell in position, working both shoes at the same time so that they match. Leave to dry.

3 Beaded shoes: String alternate turquoise and white beads on thread to fit around the front of the shoe. Tie a knot on the end of a second piece of thread. Couch between the beads. Finish with a double backstitch.

4 Thread trumpet-shaped flowers and leaves with 2 white beads to decorate the shoes' center fronts.

5 At the back, make a loop from 3 turquoise and 4 white beads.

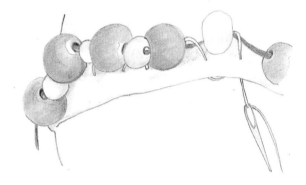

Using a second thread, couch down between each bead

Thread on the beads and catch the thread into the back of the shoe to make a loop

Paint jobs
Summer shoes can also be decorated with painted designs. Fabric paints are available in squeeze bottles and tubes – you just apply the patterns in squirls and blobs and leave to dry. Fluorescent and glitter paints are ideal for putting designs on evening boots and shoes. Sequins can be stuck on for sparkle.

Buttoned up

Brighten up your casual clothes with a set of flower buttons. They're fun to make and fun to wear so just pick your favorite flowers and get rolling. Children will love them!

Oven bake materials
Modeling clay in red, pink, white, green, yellow, orange and blue
Craft knife
Large needle
Rolling pin
Plastic pastry board

Preparation
1 Make a card template of a leaf by drawing around a small real leaf on thin card; carefully cut out.

2 Mix some green and white clay by twisting and rolling them together to marbled green.

Making the leaves
3 Roll out the clay to a thickness of about ⅛in (3mm). Place the template on the clay and, using a craft knife, cut around. Make as many leaves as you require.

4 For a realistic touch, press the real leaf onto the shape, so that the veined structure of the leaf is transferred to the surface of the clay. Use the large needle to make 2 holes in the center of each leaf.

5 Place the leaves on a sheet of oven-proof paper on a cookie sheet. Bake at 275°F (gas mark 1) for 20–30 minutes.

Making the flowers
6 Tulips: Draw a tulip shape on thin cardboard (refer to the diagram for the shape). Cut out for a template.

7 Mix red and a little orange clay together to give a marbled effect. Roll out to a thickness of about ⅛in (3mm).

Use a needle to pierce 2 holes in the button

Cut tulip shapes from clay

8 Use the cardboard template to cut out as many tulips as you need. Pierce 2 center holes. Bake as for leaves.

9 White daisies: Roll white clay with your hand to form a long thin rope. Cut into 5 pieces each ¼in (6mm) long. Roll the pieces into small teardrop-shapes then flatten slightly to form petals.

10 Arrange the 5 petals together to form the daisy flower. Gently roll over the surface to level the petals and help to join them together.

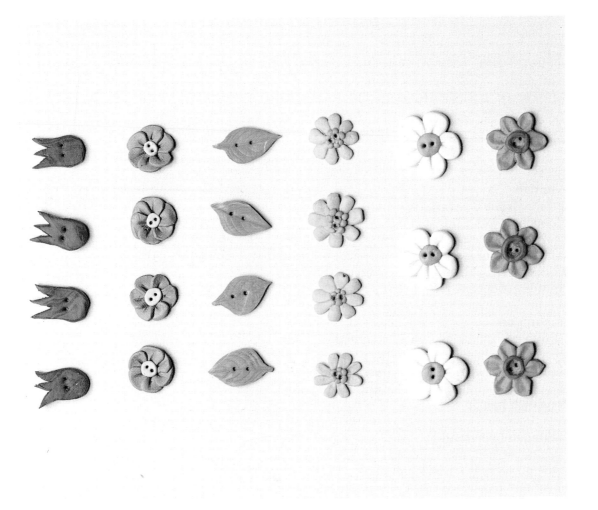

11 Mix a little yellow and orange clay together to make pale orange. Form into small balls and place one in the center of each flower. Roll over to flatten the center and help secure it.

12 Gently press the back of the craft knife into each petal to form a shape. Pierce 2 center holes. Bake as for the leaves.

13 Small yellow daisies: Make these in a similar way to the white daisies, but with 8 small petals. Make the centers from a mixture of orange and yellow clays.

14 Daffodils: Mix yellow and orange clay together. Make 6 petals as for the white daisies but with slightly pointed tips. Join the petals together as for the daisies.

15 Roll out small balls of orange. Flatten into the center of each flower. Roll a very thin rope of orange; cut into small pieces and form into circles to form the raised centers of each flower. Gently roll a toothpick across each petal to make it concave. Pierce 2 holes. Bake as for the leaves.

16 Mauve and pink flowers: Mix a little red and blue clay together with some pink to make a mauve color. Roll out the clay thinly and make 6 petals as for the white daisies but make them slightly wider. Join the petals together by slightly overlapping the edges.

17 Mix pink and white clay together and form into small balls. Flatten into the center of each flower. Pierce 2 center holes. Bake as for the leaves.

Spinning in the wind

Have some fun on a windy day with a paper windmill. It's just a square of paper cut and twisted into an aerodynamic shape. When the wind blows just watch it spin!

Materials
Posterboard in 2 contrasting colors
Wooden dowel, 12in (30cm) long, ½in (12mm) in diameter
Nail, 1½in (4cm) long
Wooden beads, ½in (12mm) diameter
Colored cellophane tape

Preparation
1 From posterboard, cut a 10in (25cm) square. Draw lines diagonally from corner to corner. Mark 1¼in (3cm) from the center point along each line. Cut from the corners along each line up to mark.

Making the windmill
2 Using the nail, push a hole in the center of the posterboard. Mark and make a hole ¾in (18mm) from each corner in the middle of each right-hand section.

3 Using pinking shears, cut a 2in (5cm)-diameter circle from contrast posterboard. Make a hole in the center of the circle.

4 Thread the nail through 1 bead, then through the posterboard circle, then through the hole in each section of the windmill in turn, bending the sails to the middle. Then push the nail through the center hole in the posterboard, through the second bead and hammer the nail into the dowel, 1in (2.5cm) from one end.

5 Decorate the wooden stick with strips of colored cellophane tape.

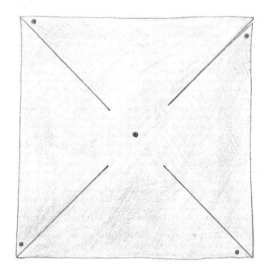

Pierce holes ¾in (18mm) from the corner in the right hand sections

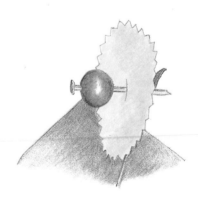

Thread the nail first through the bead, then the posterboard circle, then through the corner hole

Box of flowers

Press a selection of simple garden flowers and then use them to decorate a plain whitewood box. Once the arrangement has been sealed with varnish it will last for years.

Materials
Small whitewood trinket box
Flowers for pressing
White blotting paper or paper towel
Clear glue
Spray varnish
Giftwrap paper (optional)

Preparation
1 Cut the flower heads from the chosen plants in the morning after the dew has dried. Lay them between two sheets of white blotting paper (or pieces of soft paper towel). Place the blotting paper sheets under a pile of heavy books and leave for 4–5 weeks. (Alternatively, a flower press can be used.)

When spraying varnish, stand the piece on a small support and place it inside a large cardboard box. Turn the support to spray on all sides. A cardboard box also makes a good drying place for varnished pieces and protects the surface from dust while they are drying.

Decorating the box
2 Remove the pressed flowers. Holding the flowers in tweezers, touch a dot of glue to the back of each flower and spread with a fingertip. Position them over the box lid in a pleasing, overlapping arrangement. Position individual flowers around the sides of the box. Leave to dry.

Hold flowers in tweezers to prevent them from becoming damaged

3 Spray the entire box with varnish, leave to dry. Spray the box 8 or 9 times, leaving the varnish to dry completely between each coat.

Lining the box
4 Use giftwrap paper to line the box and lid. Cut the box bottom and lid pieces first, adding ¼in (6mm) all around. Snip into the edges and glue the pieces in position, pressing the excess on to the sides. Next, cut the long side strips, adding ¼in (6mm) to the ends. Glue in place. Cut the short side pieces exactly to size and glue in place.

Autumn beauty

An everlasting decoration made from dried flowers and grasses. Choose flowers in colors to suit your decor and add nuts, wooden beads and small bunches of raffia, for texture.

Materials
Florists' styrofoam ball, 4in (10cm) diameter
Plastic flower pot to fit inside an earthenware pot
Decorator's plaster
Wooden dowel, 11in (28cm) long, ½in (12mm) diameter
Selection of dried flowers and grasses
Walnuts
Florists' wire
Bronze-colored spray paint
Skein of raffia
Clear glue
Dried moss
Large wooden beads

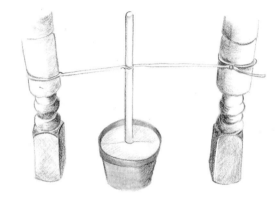

Support the wood dowel on string tied around the middle while the filler is drying

Preparation

1 Mix sufficient plaster with water to fill the plastic pot. The mixture should be thick. Spoon into the pot and stand the dowel in the center. Leave to dry. Spray the pot and the dowel stick bronze.

2 Spread the top of the dowel with glue and push on the foam ball.

3 Push the nuts onto a short length of florists' wire. Spray bronze.

4 Cut stems to about 4in (10cm), push flowers and grasses and the wired walnuts into the styrofoam ball. Wind some raffia around your fingers. Bend a short length of wire over the center and twist ends together. Open out the raffia. Push the wire ends into the ball. Push wooden beads onto the grass stalks.

5 Add to the arrangement, inserting pieces of dried moss until the ball is completely covered.

Make wire stems on raffia, push a wire stem into the nuts and push beads onto stalks

6 Mask the top of the earthenware pot with a piece of paper and spray the pot bronze. Fit the plastic pot inside the earthenware pot.

Pretty pomanders

Hang aromatic dried oranges studded with cloves in the closet for a natural perfume. Pomanders are traditional presents, particular at Christmas, and their spicy scent makes them a household favorite.

Materials

Masking tape ¾in (18mm) wide
Thin skinned oranges
Whole cloves
1tsp (5ml) ground cinnamon
1tsp (5ml) ground allspice
2oz (60g) orris root powder
Double-edged lace, ¾in (18mm) wide, 20in (50cm) long
Embroidered ribbon ⅜in (9mm) wide, 22in (56cm) long
Pearlized glass-headed pins

Preparation

1 Cut and pin masking tape to go around the orange, a second strip at right angles to the first, to quarter it. Pierce holes in the orange ¼in (6mm) apart. Push cloves into the holes to fill the quarter sections between the tapes. Remove the masking tapes.

2 Mix the orris root powder, allspice and cinnamon together in a plastic bag. Toss the orange in the mixture inside the bag. Remove and shake off excess powder.

3 Wrap the orange in tissue paper and leave in a dry, warm place for 2–3 weeks to dry out.

Making the pomander

4 Cut the lace in half. Wrap each piece around the orange in the channels left by the tape. Overlap the lace ends and pin or glue to secure.

5 Beginning at the top, wrap the ribbon around the pomander placing it centrally over the lace. Pin or glue at the top and the cross-over point at the base. If the pomander is to be hung, form a loop at the top with ribbon and hold in place with glass-headed pins.

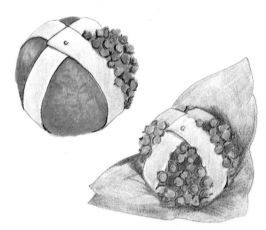

Pin tape around the orange, push cloves into the pierced holes. After tossing the orange in orris powder and spices, wrap and leave to dry

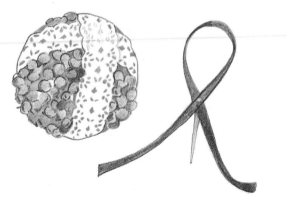

Tape lace and pin ribbons around the orange. Make a ribbon loop to pin to the top if the pomander is to be hung

All tied up

Create an unusual picture by weaving glossy embroidery thread around bead-tipped pins. Match the thread colors to your decor for an harmonious effect.

Materials
Cork tile, 8in (20cm) square
Piece of fabric 20 × 10in (50 × 25cm)
Iron-on interfacing 20 × 10in (50 × 25cm)
64 small nails
64 blue beads
Embroidery thread in blue, pink and
  mauve
Curtain ring, ¾in (18mm) diameter
Glue

Preparation
1 Fuse the interfacing to the wrong side of the fabric. Cut the fabric in 2 pieces each 10in (25cm) square.

2 Glue the cork tile to the interfaced side of the fabric, centering it. Trim off the corners diagonally. Turn the excess fabric to the wrong side and glue in place. Place second piece of fabric right side up, over the other side of the tile, fold under the raw edges and glue in place. Slipstitch all around on the edges.

3 Sew the curtain ring to the back of the picture 1½in (4cm) from top edge and in the middle.

Using pink thread, work each corner from nail 1 to nail 16

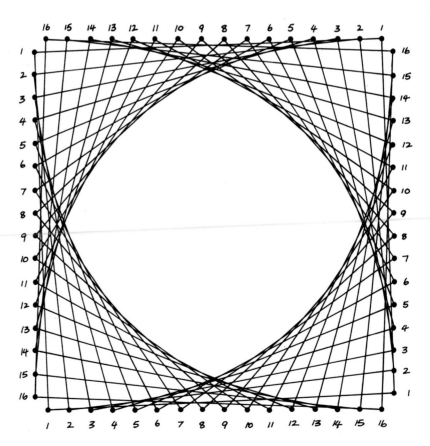

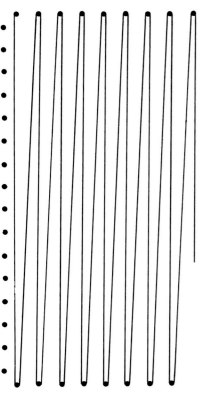

Making the picture

4 Slip 16 beads on 16 nails and hammer the nails into the tile ¾in (18mm) from the edges spacing them ⅜in (9mm) apart. Work the other 3 sides in the same way.

5 Using the blue thread, lace round the nails from top to bottom across the tile.

6 Working first with pink thread then with mauve, work each corner from nail 1 to nail 16, as shown in the diagram.

7 Knot the threads around the last nails. Trim ends.

Wind blue thread around the nails from top to bottom

Pots of style

Treat your windows to a new look with a row of pretty flower pots.
Cover them with fabric to match the curtains or cushions.
Complete the look with a tartan bow.

Materials
Earthenware flower pot
White liquid glue
Cotton print furnishing fabric
Nylon taffeta ribbon in a tartan pattern

Preparation
1 Make a small mark on the inside rim of the flower pot. Lay the pot down on a sheet of paper with mark over the paper. Holding a pencil against the rim, move the pot along the paper, until you come around to mark again. Repeat at the base of the pot. Join the two curved lines with straight lines.

2 Cut out the shape, adding $\frac{3}{8}$in (9mm) for overlap on one side edge and $\frac{3}{4}$in (18mm) on the top and base edges. Using the pattern, cut out from fabric. (Make sure that any linear pattern runs straight across, or down, the fabric.)

3 Seal the outside of the flower pot with water-diluted white liquid glue. Leave to dry.

Spread the ribbon on paper and coat with diluted white liquid glue

4 Coat the pot with white liquid glue again and apply fabric all around, with the overlap even at the top and base. Overlap the side edges trimming off any excess that is required for a neat finish.

Roll the pot along the paper and pencil along the rim. Repeat at the base

Tie a bow around the flower pot while the glue is still wet

5 Snip into the overlaps at the top and base. Glue the overlap to the inside of the top rim. Glue the bottom overlap to the underside of the pot. Leave to dry.

6 Dilute more white liquid glue to a thin cream consistency. Coat the ribbon. Tie the ribbon around the pot while the glue is still wet and tie a bow. Leave to dry. Trim the ribbon ends into 'fishtails'.

Light the way

Decorate a plain white lampshade with fabric paint designs and bring the room to life with an attractive new look.

Materials

Plain white lampshade, 7in (18cm) high, 12in (30cm)-diameter base, 4in (10cm)-diameter top
Water-based fabric paints
Fine-tipped paint brush
Fabric protector spray

Preparation

1 Make a paper pattern from the lampshade following the technique described for the flowerpot on page 102 stage 1.

Working the design

2 Trace the pattern on pages 108–9, repeating the motifs all around the shade. The small motifs go around the upper edge. The butterflies are set at random.

3 Tape the edges of the paper pattern together and tape inside the shade, lining up the seam of the shade with the join in the paper.

This design would be ideal for embroidery and could be used to make curtain ties and a cushion to match the lampshade. The design could be worked entirely in satin stitch or long and short stitch, or the larger shapes could be outlined in backstitch. You might also try painting the design on the wrong side of fabric for making your own lampshade, using fabric paints, and then embroider the outlines of the flowers, leaves and butterflies on the right side. This would produce the effect of shadow embroidery.

Tape the traced pattern inside the shade, then trace the lines onto the shade

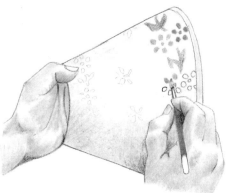

Paint the design working towards you so that you do not smudge your work

4 Place the shade over a low-watt light bulb and trace the motifs onto the shade, using a soft pencil. Remove the pattern.

5 Mix the fabric paints and, using one color at a time, paint the design. Work in one direction around the shade to avoid

smudging the painted areas already worked. Paint the leaves first, then the flowers and lastly the butterflies. Leave to dry completely.

6 With a soft eraser remove any pencil marks that still show on the right side of the shade. Finally spray the shade with a fabric protector.

Trace the lampshade motifs given here.
Repeat the motifs around the lampshade
pattern.

Summer baskets

Transform simple wicker baskets into decorative features to display around the home. Fill them with dried flowers, foliage, pine cones or even shiny red apples. All you need is a little fabric and some paint.

Materials
Wicker baskets with handles
Spray paint (flat or gloss)
Printed cotton fabric 36 × 20in (90 × 50cm)
White liquid glue
A few fabric flowers (optional)

Preparation
1 Spray-paint the baskets.

2 Cut 2 widths of fabric each 4in (10cm) deep. Stitch into a tube, right sides facing. Press the seam open. Turn to the right side. Turn the raw edge on one end of the tube and slipstitch over the opposite end.

3 Run a gathering thread through center of the fabric ring and pull up to fit the top of the basket. Sew in place through the wicker. Brush the fabric with diluted white liquid glue and leave to dry.

4 Cut a piece of fabric 36 × 6in (90 × 15cm). Press in the raw edges and tie into a bow around the basket handle. Stiffen the fabric with white liquid glue. Decorate, if desired.

Gather the ring around the middle

Baskets for gifts
You can use the method described here to make attractive and useful baskets for bathroom accessories. If the basket is to be used for soaps it is a good idea to put a lining into the base. Stand the basket on a sheet of paper and trace around the base. Cut out for a pattern and cut the shape twice from fabric, adding ½in (12mm) all around for a seam allowance. Using the paper pattern, cut the same shape in thin batting. Baste the batting to the wrong side of one fabric circle, baste the second circle to the first, right sides facing. Machine-stitch all around, leaving a gap of about 4in (10cm) for turning. Turn right side out and close the gap with hemming or slipstitches. Fit the lining into the basket. If you like, you could catch the layers of the lining together with short lengths of very narrow satin ribbon, tying the ends in bows.

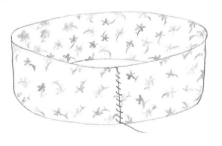

Stitch the 2 pieces of fabric into a tube, turn to the right side and sew one end over the other

Greetings!

Send a very special message with a handmade card, cleverly woven with ribbons and framed in lace.

Materials
Card blanks with an oval opening
Stiff paper
¼in (6mm)-wide ribbon in colors of your
    choice
Lace edging, ⅝in (15mm) wide, 14in (36cm)
    long
Glue
Double-sided clear cellophane tape
Small natural sponge
Water-based paints

Making the cards
1 Mix the paint and dab over the front and back of the card, using the sponge. Leave to dry.

2 Cut a piece of paper to the same size as the card front. Place it behind the card front and pencil around the oval opening.

3 Cut ribbons to fit across the oval diagonally plus about ¼in (6mm) at each end.

4 Tape the 'warp' ribbons down first, edges touching, in a color arrangement of your choice.

Ribbon weaving would also make a very pretty Valentine's Day card. Use very narrow ribbons – ⅛ or ¼in wide (3 or 6mm) and in a range of different red colors – bright red, scarlet and crimson. Cut a heart shape from the front of a card blank. Glue the ribbon weaving behind the heart then back it with white paper. Write a loving message inside.

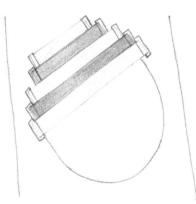

Tape down the warp ribbons first

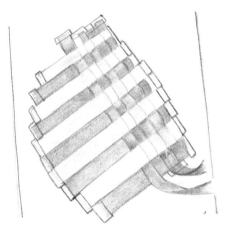

Weave ribbons through, over one, under one and tape down

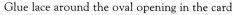

Glue lace around the oval opening in the card

5 Weave the 'weft' ribbons over and under the 'warp' ribbons, taping down at both ends.

6 Glue lace edging around the oval opening, overlapping the edges at the bottom of the oval to neaten.

7 Using double-sided tape, fix the piece of paper with the woven ribbon oval on it behind the opening in the card front, positioning it exactly in the oval opening.

8 Fold up the card.

113

Frame up

Frame two favorite photographs side by side in an attractive fabric-covered frame. Matched to furnishings, the frame makes a pretty bedroom accessory.

Materials

Printed cotton fabric, 15in (38cm) square
Posterboard 15in (38cm) square
Iron-on lightweight interfacing, 15in (38cm) square
Fabric glue
Clear glue
Ribbon, $\frac{1}{4}$in (6mm)-wide, 4in (10cm)
Narrow braid, 25in (64cm)
2 small ribbon roses
Piece of acetate, 9 × 6in (23 × 15cm)
Piece of white paper, 9 × 6in (23 × 15cm)
Clear cellophane tape

Preparation

1 From posterboard, cut a back and front $8\frac{3}{4}$ × 6in (22 × 15cm). Cut a spacing strip for the bottom edge $8\frac{3}{4}$ × $\frac{3}{8}$in (22cm × 9mm), two strips for the sides $5\frac{5}{8}$ × $\frac{3}{8}$in (14.5cm × 9mm) and one strip for the center $5\frac{5}{8}$in × $\frac{3}{4}$in (14.5cm × 18mm).

2 Trace the oval shape and trade down twice on to one piece of posterboard. Score around the outlines first with the tip of a craft knife, then go around again, deeper, until the posterboard is cut through cleanly.

3 Cut one stand from posterboard, following the measurements given.

Making the frame

4 Fuse the interfacing to the wrong side of the fabric. Place the stand piece of posterboard on the fabric and mark around twice. Cut out both shapes adding $\frac{3}{8}$in (9mm) all around to one of them. Glue the piece of posterboard to the center of the larger fabric shape. Turn in the side and bottom edges only and glue on the wrong side.

5 Glue one end of the ribbon to the back of the stand in the middle of the bottom edge. Glue the smaller piece of fabric over the back of the stand covering the ribbon.

6 Glue the spacing strips to the side, center and bottom edge of the frame front. Place it on the interfaced fabric and mark around. Cut out adding $\frac{3}{8}$in (9mm) all around.

Trace the oval shape and trace down twice on posterboard

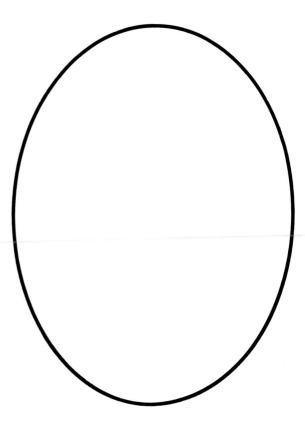

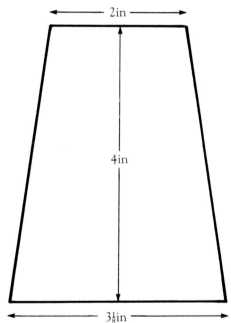

2in

4in

3⅛in

Copy this diagram on posterboard and cut out for the stand

7 Glue the posterboard centrally to the wrong side of the fabric. Turn the edges to the wrong side and glue in place, making neat corners. Cut out around the ovals, ⅜in (9mm) from the posterboard edges, snip into the fabric and glue down on the wrong side.

8 Place the stand centrally on the frame back and pencil along the top edge. Cut along the pencilled line to make a slit. Cover the frame back with fabric in the same way as for the front. Cut the fabric along the slit.

9 Position the stand on the back, the bottom edges level. Pull the raw edges of fabric on the top edge of the stand through the slit to the wrong side of the back. Tape down. Glue the remaining end of ribbon to the wrong side of the back. Cut and glue a piece of white paper to wrong side of the frame back.

10 Glue the front frame to the back, spreading glue along the spacing strips only, leaving the top edge open.

11 Cut 2 pieces of acetate each 5½ × 3½in (13 × 8cm) and slot into each side of frame behind the oval openings.

12 Glue braid around the ovals bringing the ends together at the bottom of the oval. Glue a small ribbon rose over the join in the braid.

Ball of roses

Create a beautiful decoration from ribbon roses pushed into a ball.
Add a hanging ribbon and perhaps ribbon streamers.

Materials

White styrofoam ball, 4in (10cm) in
  diameter
Pastel colored single-face satin ribbons, 1½
  (4cm), 1in (2.5cm) and ⅛in (3mm) wide
Stem wire and florist's wire
Florist's green stem binding tape
Silk or plastic rose leaves

Preparation

1 For the large roses cut 24in (60cm)
lengths of ribbon, for the small roses cut
14in (36cm) lengths of ribbon. Bend over
one end of a stem wire. Thread the florist's
wire into the hook and wind it around to
fasten.

Making a rose

2 Take the end of the ribbon and fold it
over the top of the wire hook, secure with
florist's wire. Pull the ribbon out to one
side and wrap it around the covered wire
3–4 times and secure with wire.

3 To form the petals, fold the ribbon
diagonally away from the flower head, then
turn the rose center to the middle of the
fold. Continue turning the rose until the
ribbon is straight again. Continue forming
petals until you reach the end of the
ribbon, winding the florist's wire around
the base to hold the petals in place.

4 To complete the rose, bring the ribbon
end down to the bottom of the flower and
bind it firmly. Cut off the wire.

5 Trim the stem wire to 2in (5cm). Bind
the stem with florist's tape. Begin at the
base of the flower, sticking it firmly in
place. Gently stretching the tape, turn the
rose until the whole stem is covered. Trim
the end.

Making ribbon loops

6 Cut an 18in (45cm) length of ⅛in (3mm)-
wide ribbon. Make a hooked stem wire as
for the roses. Form the end of the ribbon
into a loop about 4½in (11.5cm) long and
bind it to the stem.

7 Make 3–4 more loops, binding each one
in place. Trim the stem and cover with tape
in the same way as for the rose.

Making the ball

8 Using a knitting needle, make a hole
through the center of the styrofoam ball.
Bend a hook on a stem wire. Push the
other end through the ball. Trim the wire
end, bend a hook.

9 Push roses and ribbon loops into the ball
to cover it. Push leaves in between the
roses. Tie a hanging loop of 1½in (4cm)-
wide ribbon to the top hook. If you like,
knot streamers of narrow ribbon to the
bottom hook.

Fold and wire the ribbon over the hook on
the stem wire

Bind ribbon loops to cover the hook on the stem wire

Push a long, hooked stem wire through the ball, bend the end into a hook

117

More Needlecrafts

Hanging fragrance

Bring the scents of summer into your wardrobe with these pretty fabric-covered hangers. Make lacy potpourri sachets, to tie to the hook with satin ribbon.

Materials
Wooden coat hanger
Batting
Floral print fabric
Net (for inside the sachet)
Cotton lawn for the sachet
Lavender or potpourri
$\frac{5}{8}$in (15mm)-wide lace edging
1in (2.5cm)-wide double-edged fine lace
1in (2.5cm)-wide double-edged heavy lace
$\frac{1}{4}$in (6mm)-wide feather edge satin ribbon
$\frac{1}{2}$in (12mm)-wide satin ribbon

Preparation
1 Wrap the hanger in batting and stitch in place.

2 Cut and make a rouleau strip (see Better Techniques) as long as the hanger hook, closing one end. Thread over the hook and sew to the batting at the base of the hook.

Covering the hanger
3 Cut a strip of the print fabric twice the length of the hanger by $6\frac{1}{4}$in (16cm). Press a $\frac{5}{8}$in (15mm) hem on both long edges. Fold in half with right sides together, pin and stitch ends. Turn to right side.

4 Fold the strip and mark the center. Using a doubled thread, work a row of gathering along the folded edges. Wind the thread ends around a pin in a figure-of-eight. Work gathering along the top edge also, joining the folded edges together up to the center.

5 Insert one end of the hanger and pull up the threads to fit. Fasten off the top threads at the hook, stitching through the rouleau covering the hook to secure.

6 Work gathering along the remaining top edge of the hanger cover in the same way. Fasten.

Sachet
7 Cut a piece of lawn 7 × 5in (17.5 × 12.5cm). Turn double hems on the short sides. Stitch. Lay the fabric flat. Stitch lace edging over the hemmed edges. Stitch the heavy lace across the middle. Stitch the fine double-edged lace between the middle and edges.

8 Fold the sachet right sides facing, pin and stitch the long seam. Turn right side out.

9 Make a net insert by cutting a $4\frac{3}{4}$in (12cm) square. Fold in half and stitch the edges together. Gather up one end and fasten off. Fill with lavender or potpourri, gather up the remaining end and fasten.

Follow this arrangement for the lace decoration on the sachet

10 Place the sachet inside the outer sachet. Gather up both ends, tie with the narrow ribbon and finish with a bow. Cut a 7in (18cm)-length of narrow ribbon. Fold in half and sew the ends to the inside top of the sachet. Loop the sachet over the hanger hook.

11 Tie ½in (12mm)-wide ribbon around the hook into a bow, holding the sachet ribbon in place.

One for the pot

Bouquet garni sachets make ideal gifts for cooks. Store them in a pretty vinyl holder to hang beside the stove.

Materials
Patterned vinyl cloth 25 × 10in (52 × 25cm)
Bias binding, 1¼yd × ½in (1.20m × 12mm)
Muslin, 30 × 12in (76 × 30cm) (makes 10)
Dried bouquet garni herbs (thyme, parsley,
 bay leaf)
Strong white thread
Curtain ring, ½in (12mm) diameter

Preparation
1 From the vinyl cut two 8in (20cm) squares.

2 Cut another square for the front pocket piece, cutting one corner off diagonally.

Making the holder
3 Bind the top of the pocket with bias binding.

4 Place the 2 squares with wrong sides together with the pocket on top. Bind around the outer edge, catching in the pocket edges.

5 Sew a curtain ring to the back of the top corner.

Sachets
6 From muslin, cut 6in (15cm)-diameter circles using pinking shears.

7 With strong thread, gather around the circle, 1in (2.5cm) from the outer edge. Place a small amount of dried herbs in the center of each circle. Pull up both ends of thread together and tie. Tie threads together again, 7in (18cm) from the last knot, to form a loop. This loop will slip over the handle when the bouquet garni is in the saucepan.

Bind the top of the pocket with bias binding

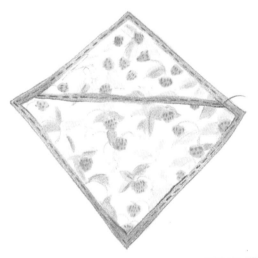

Bind around the outer edges of the squares, catching in the pocket.

Working with vinyl
Vinyl is easy to cut out and handles just like any other fabric. Some people, however, find it tricky to stitch. If the fabric sticks to the base plate, slip tissue paper between the vinyl and the machine.

Memories

Decorate the covers of a plain album with silk and beads and make it extra-special for wedding memories or for baby's first pictures.

Materials
Album to cover, 11 × 9in (26 × 23cm)
Plain silk fabric, 38 × 13in (96.5 × 33cm)
Quilted padding, 20 × 13in (50 × 33cm)
Gold metallic machine thread
Matching thread
Small gold beads
Pearl button

Preparation
1 Cut 2 pieces of silk, each $19\frac{5}{8} \times 12\frac{1}{2}$in (50 × 31cm) and a piece of quilted padding the same size. Fuse the padding to the wrong side of one piece of silk.

2 Put the gold thread on the bobbin of the sewing machine. Following the pre-printed lines, quilt the fabric.

Making the album cover
3 Make a 5in (12.5cm) long strip of silk fabric rouleau for the fastening loop (refer to Better Techniques).

4 Sew a gold bead at each intersection of the quilting.

5 Cut 2 cover sleeves from silk, each $12\frac{1}{2} \times 8\frac{1}{4}$ (31 × 21cm). Turn a double $\frac{1}{4}$in (6mm)-wide hem on one long edge. Pin and stitch.

6 Baste the rouleau loop centrally on the back edge of the quilted fabric.

7 Place a sleeve to each end of the quilted fabric, right sides together and raw edges matching. Pin the second piece of silk on top. Stitch around, leaving one end open. Turn to the right side.

8 Slip the album covers into the sleeves. Sew the button to the front of the cover to correspond with the rouleau loop.

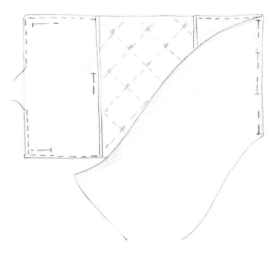

Place the sleeves in position, pin the silk fabric lining on top

Roses and pearls
For a different decoration, make a spray of cream and white ribbon roses. Using 1in (2.5cm) ribbon, fold roses as described on page 116 but catching the base of the rose together with stitches instead of using a wire stem. Fold ribbon leaves from 2in (5cm) lengths of ribbon. Sew the roses and leaves to the album cover in a pleasing arrangement. Sew 2 or 3 pearl beads to the rose centers. Sew a few more pearl beads around the arrangement. Stems can be made by catching down very narrow ribbons.

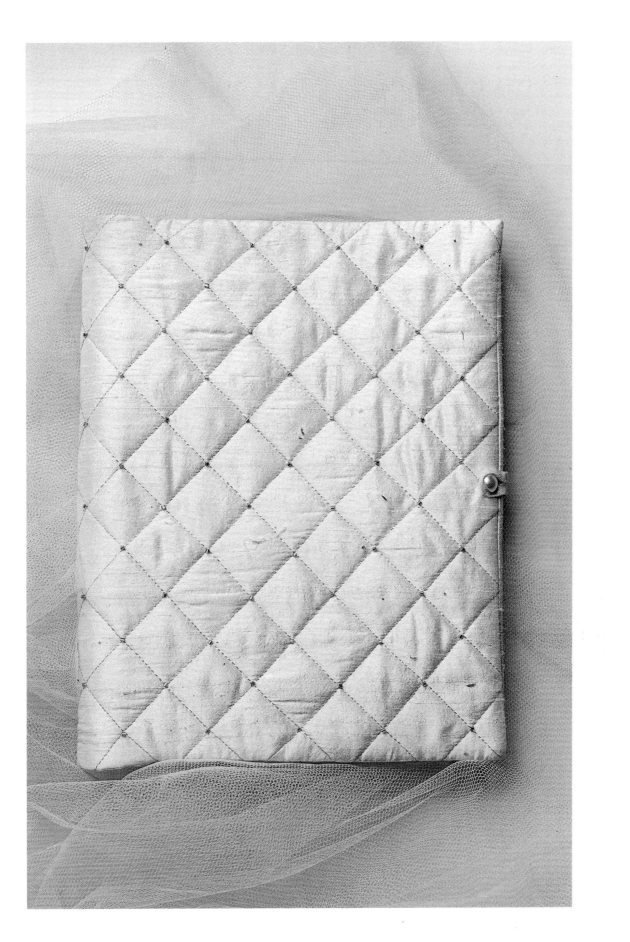

Bathing beauties

Plain towels get a bright new look with smart jacquard ribbon and pretty lace trims. They are simple to sew and the perfect complement to a stylish bathroom.

Materials
Plain towels
Easy-care jacquard woven ribbons, 1in and
⅜in (2.5cm and 9mm) wide
Doubled edged lace ⅝in (15mm) wide
Lace edging ⅜in (9mm) wide

Preparation
1 Peach towel: Cut 4 pieces of the lace edging to the width of the towel plus ½in (12mm). Cut a piece of the wider ribbon to the same length.

2 Baste 2 lengths of lace at each end of the towel (over the embossed area) facing outwards and ¾in (18mm) apart. Tuck under ¼in (6mm) at each end to neaten.

Working the design
3 Baste the ribbon between the lace edgings, neatening the ends as before.

4 Machine-stitch down the edges of the ribbon catching in the lace edging on either side as you stitch. Make sure you stitch in the same direction on both edges to prevent puckering.

5 Decorate both ends of the towel in the same way.

6 Blue towel: Cut 2 pieces of double-edged lace to the width of the towel plus ½in (12mm). Place one piece at each end of the towel over the embossed area, tucking under ¼in (6mm) at each end to neaten. Pin, baste and stitch, down the middle of the lace.

7 Cut 4 pieces of the narrow jacquard ribbon to the towel width plus ½in (12mm). Position a ribbon either side of the lace, tucking them under the lace edges. Tuck the ends under to neaten. Pin, baste and stitch in place down both edges of the ribbons.

8 Work both ends of the towel in the same way.

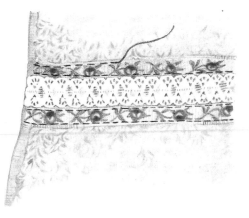

Position the ribbons either side of the lace

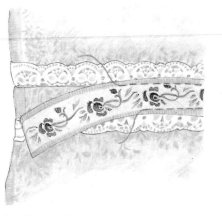

Stitch the ribbon between the strips of lace

Window style

Honeycomb curtain heading tape is ideal for making attractive tie-backs. Either make them in the same fabric as the curtains or choose a patterned fabric to match with a plain fabric. They are so simple they could be made in an evening.

Materials
Furnishing fabric, 48 × 15½in (120 × 39cm)
Smocked honeycomb-style curtain heading
 tape, 3yd (2.8m) long
Curtain rings, ½in (12mm) diameter

Preparation
1 Cut 2 strips of fabric each 48 × 7¾in (120 × 19.5cm). Turn in 1½in (4cm) on both long edges and press. Turn in 1in (2.5cm) at each short end, mitering the corners.

Making the tie-backs
2 Cut 2 pieces of heading tape to the same length as the fabric strips, plus 2in (5cm). Knot the cords at one end.

3 Turn under the tape ends, 1in (2.5cm). Pin and baste to the wrong side of the fabric, centring the tape.

4 Machine-stitch 4 rows across the tape and then down the short ends.

5 Pull up the cords until a smocked effect is formed. Tie the cords together, wind up the ends.

6 Sew a curtain ring to each end of the tie-backs. These can hold the wound-up cords at the same time.

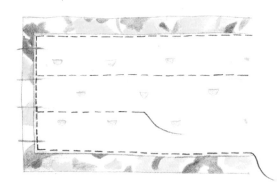

Work 4 rows of machine-stitching across the tape, then stitch down the short sides

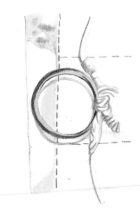

Wind up the cords, push through the rings to hold them securely in place

Guard that door

Sew a smiling crocodile to guard your door against drafts. He can follow you around the house to keep each room warm and cozy.

Materials
Printed cotton fabric, 40 × 18in
   (102 × 45cm)
Wide green rickrack braid, 28in (70cm)
Washable polyester toy filling

Narrow green rickrack braid, 30in (76cm)
12in (30cm) squares of felt, emerald
   green, yellow; scraps of dark green, pink
Pair of joggle eyes, ¾in (18mm) diameter

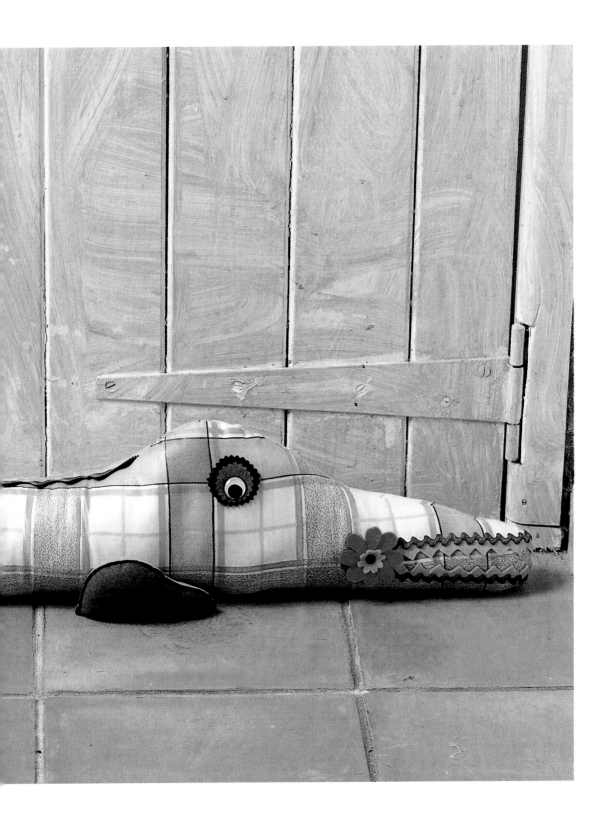

Preparation

1 On graph paper draw the shapes for the main body and the flower from the graph below.

2 Using the paper pattern, cut 2 body pieces from printed fabric. Cut 4 green and 4 yellow felt feet. Cut the emerald green inner eyes and dark green outer eyes from felt using pinking shears. Cut the flower petals from pink felt with the inner flower in yellow felt. Cut a small green felt circle for the flower center.

Making the crocodile

3 Pin the wide rickrack braid to the right side along the top edges of one body piece. Place the bodies with right sides together. Pin, baste and stitch, all around catching in the braid and leaving an opening along the base edge. Turn the body to the right side. Fill the crocodile firmly. Turn in the opening edges and slipstitch together to close.

Cut 'v's into one edge of the yellow felt strips

4 Stick the joggle eyes to the inner, green eyes, then stick to the outer, dark green eyes. Stick the completed eyes on either side of head.

Draw the graph pattern on squared paper (scale 1 sq = 1in (2.5cm)

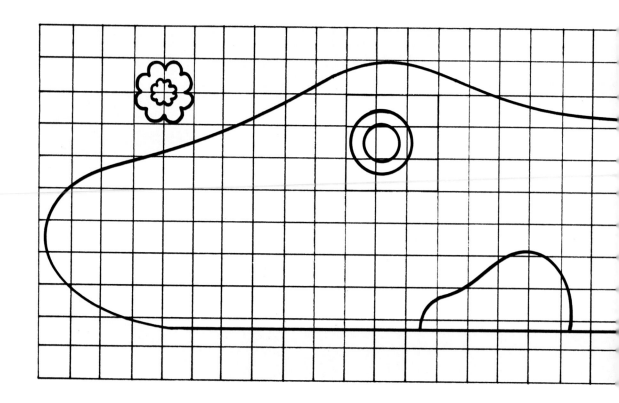

5 For the mouth, cut 2 strips of yellow felt 15 × 1in (38 × 2.5cm). Cut one edge of each piece into 'Vs'. Glue to the head around the mouth with the points facing inwards for teeth. Glue the narrow, green rickrack braid round the upper edge of the felt mouth.

6 Make up the flower, glue to one side of the mouth.

7 Stitch the feet together in pairs of green and yellow. Fill slightly. Sew the legs to either side of the body.

Crocodile toy
You can use the basic crocodile pattern to make a long toy for a small child. Children find these fun to play with and drape them around their necks – or curl them into a 'nest' for a quick nap. Scraps of cotton fabric can be used. Cut 14in (35cm) squares of contrasting fabrics. Seam together to make a strip about 36in (90cm) long. Join the long side to make a tube. Cut 2 crocodile heads from fabric, join (inserting rickrack braid), then sew the head to the tube. Sew on eyes and mouth. Stuff the crocodile from the tail end, keeping the stuffing soft and flexible. Trim the end to a narrow tail, turn in the edges and slipstitch to close, pushing in a little more stuffing. Add felt feet if desired.

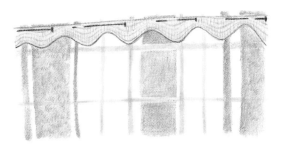

Pin the rickrack braid along the top edge of the body piece

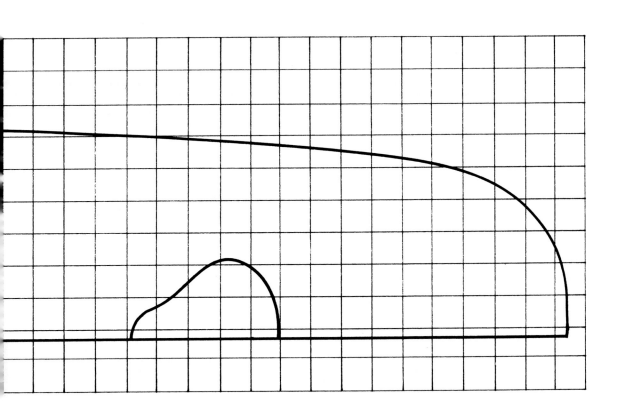

Roll up, roll up!

Bread and rolls keep warm in this pretty pocketed basket lining. Match the lining to your tablecloth and napkins for a coordinated effect. It can also be used to display fruit, such as oranges, peaches, apricots, pears or apples.

Materials
Printed cotton fabric, 36 × 12in (90 × 30cm)
Gingham check fabric, 36 × 12in
  (90 × 30cm)
Rickrack braid ½in (12mm) wide, 3yd
  (2.7m) long
2 snaps
12in (30cm)-diameter basket

Preparation
1 From each of the fabrics cut out 3 circles each 12in (30cm) in diameter (6 circles in total).

2 Pin and baste rickrack braid around 3 circles of the same fabric ½in (12mm) from the edge. Place the circles together in pairs, one print to one gingham, wrong sides facing.

3 Pin, baste and stitch all around, leaving an opening. Trim the seam allowance and turn right side out. Turn in the opening edges and slipstitch to close.

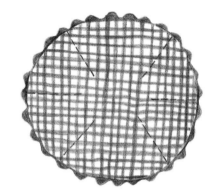

Stitch the third circle in place, between each segment to within 3in (7.5cm) of the center

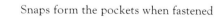

Snaps form the pockets when fastened

Stitch the 2 circles together dividing them into 6 segments

Try making the basket lining from spotted voile or lawn, trimming the edges with narrow cotton lace. Interline the circles with white cotton.

4 Place 2 circles together, gingham to gingham, pin and topstitch together stitching across the circles from side to side dividing the circle into 6 segments.

5 Add the third circle on top. Pin and stitch to the middle circle between each

segment, to within 3in (7.5cm) of the center.

6 Stitch the snaps to the top circle in adjoining segments. Fasten together across the circle, to create the pockets. Place the lining in the basket.

135

Table talk

Make tea time extra special with an appliqué tablecloth and matching napkins.

Materials
Floral fabric, 36 × 48in (90 × 1.20m)
Plain glazed cotton fabric, 2¼yd × 48in
   (2 × 1.20m)
Fusible web

Preparation
1 Roughly cut the floral motifs from the fabric. Fuse fusible web to the wrong side of each piece. Cut out the motifs closely.

Making the tablecloth
2 Cut a 48in (1.20m) square from the plain fabric. Turn a double ¼in (6mm) hem all around, mitering the corners. Pin, baste and stitch the hem.

3 Peel off the backing and position a large floral motif in each corner. Fuse in place. Add smaller motifs in between the corner motifs. Baste each in place.

4 Set your sewing machine to a close satin stitch and work around each motif.

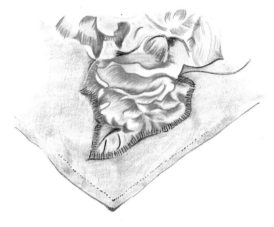

Work machine satin stitch around the motifs

Making the napkins
5 Cut six 16in (40cm) squares from the plain fabric and turn a double ¼in (6mm)-wide hem all around, mitering the corners. Pin, baste and stitch the hem.

6 Position a single floral motif in one corner of each napkin and fuse in place. Work satin stitch all around the motif.

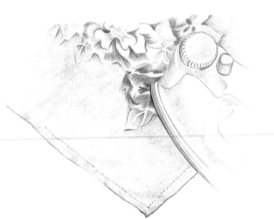

Fuse a large motif to each corner of the tablecloth

Lace appliqué
Scraps of washable lace can be used to decorate a plain, linen or cotton tablecloth. To appliqué, machine-stitch around a motif, using a medium-width satin stitch. Cut out and then sew the motifs to the cloth. To insert lace motifs and strips, baste the lace to the right side of the cloth, then zigzag machine-stitch all around the edges. On the wrong side, trim away the fabric, turn narrow hems and sew to neaten.

Good companions

Stitch a matching shower hat and a toiletry bag to hold potions and lotions. These make ideal gifts for friends of all ages.

Materials

Printed cotton fabric, 1⅛yd (1m) × 36in (90cm)

Nylon fabric, 1⅛yd (1m) × 36in (90cm)

Pre-gathered lace edging, ¾in (18mm) wide, 3½yd (3.20m) long

Elastic, ¼in (6mm) wide, 24in (60cm) long

8in (20cm) square of heavyweight iron-on interfacing

Ribbon, ¼in (6mm) wide, 2yd (1.80m) long

Preparation

1 Shower cap: Cut a 24in (60cm)-diameter circle from both the printed fabric and nylon fabric.

Making the cap

2 Pin and stitch the lace edging to right side of the fabric circle, ⅝in (15mm) from the edge. Join the lace ends to fit the circle.

3 Place the nylon circle to the right sides of the fabric circle. Pin and stitch all around, following the previous stitching line and leaving an opening for turning. Trim the seam allowance and turn to the right side. Turn in the opening edges and slipstitch together.

4 Casing: Stitch all around the cap 1½in (4cm) from the outer edge. Stitch around again ⅜in (9mm) inside the first row of stitching.

5 Cut a small slit in the casing on the nylon side. Oversew the raw edges to neaten. Measure around the head with a piece of elastic, allowing an extra ⅜in (9mm) for overlap. Fasten a safety pin to one end of the elastic and thread through the casing. Overlap the ends and oversew together. Push the join inside the casing.

6 Toiletry bag: For the sides, cut 2 pieces of fabric and 2 pieces of nylon each measuring 18 × 14in (46 × 36cm). Cut a 6in (15cm)-diameter circle from both fabric and nylon for the base. For the inside pockets, cut 2 pieces each from fabric and nylon each measuring 18 × 7in (46 × 18cm).

7 Place the fabric and nylon pocket pieces together with right sides facing. Pin and stitch the top edges. Turn right side out. Topstitch ⅜in (9mm) from the top edge.

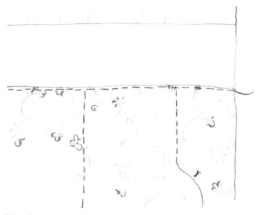

Divide the pocket into sections

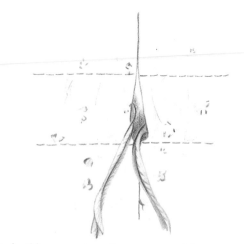

Each ribbon goes in and comes out of the same opening

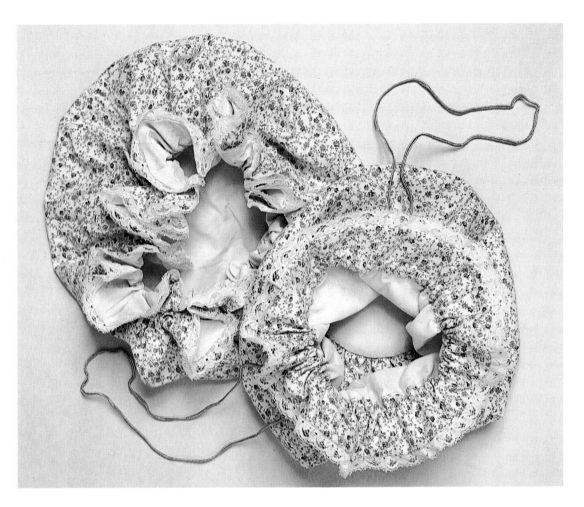

8 Place the pockets to the nylon side pieces, matching lower edges. Pin and baste together. Place the nylon side pieces right sides together. Pin and stitch the side edges. Topstitch from the pocket top to the base edges to divided each side into 3 separate pockets.

9 Place the fabric sides together with right sides facing. Pin and stitch the sides, leaving a ⅝in (15mm) opening in each side about 2¾in (7cm) from the top edge. Pin and stitch lace edging to the right side all around the top edge, joining the ends together.

10 Place the nylon lining to the fabric, right sides together. Pin and stitch around the top, following the previous stitching line. Turn to the right side. Pin and baste the bottom edges together. Topstitch around the top to form a casing.

11 Fuse the interfacing to the wrong side of the fabric base. Work a row of gathering round the bottom edges of the sides. Pull up evenly to fit the fabric base. Pin and stitch. Turn under the raw edges on the nylon base and place over fabric base, wrong sides together. Pin and topstitch all around.

12 Cut the ribbon into 2 equal lengths. Thread the first length of ribbon through the casing, going in and coming out through the same opening. Knot the ends together, push the knot into the casing. Thread the second ribbon length through the casing, going and coming out through the second opening. Knot the ends and push the knot into the casing. Pull the ribbons up from each side of the bag.

141

Great outdoors

Nothing beats eating outdoors on summer days, and with these handy picnic roll-mats you can travel – and eat – in style.

Materials
(For two roll-mats)
Checked cotton fabric, 18 × 36in
    (46 × 90cm)
Spotted green cotton fabric 24 × 36in
    (60 × 90cm)
Plain yellow cotton fabric, 26 × 12in
    (65 × 30cm)
Lightweight polyester batting 36 × 12in
    (90 × 30cm)
Heavyweight iron-on interfacing, 36 × 12in
    (90 × 30cm)
Elastic, ¾in (18mm) wide, 12in (30cm) long

Preparation
1 From checked fabric, cut 1 piece
18 × 12in (46 × 30cm) for the back and 1
piece 8½ × 12in (21 × 30cm) for the inside
center.

2 From plain yellow fabric, cut out 2
pieces each 6¼ × 12in (16 × 30cm) for the
inside pieces.

Making the roll-up
3 Cut a piece of interfacing the same size as
the back and fuse to the wrong side of the
checked fabric.

4 Strap holders: Cut 2 strips of checked
fabric each 7 × 2½in (17.5 × 6cm). Fold each
in half lengthwise right sides facing. Stitch
on the long edges taking a ¼in (6mm) seam.
Turn right side out, press.

5 Cut the elastic in half. Thread one piece
of the elastic through the strap, pin the
ends. Make up the second strap in the
same way.

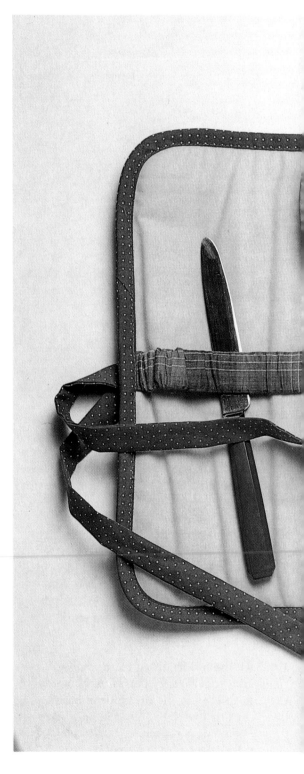

6 Pin one end of each strap to the middle of the yellow side pieces. Turn under the long edges of the checked center piece, press and overlap the yellow pieces at each side. Pin, baste and topstitch in place, catching in the end of the strap.

7 Cut a piece of batting the same size as the inside of the roll and pin and baste to the wrong side. Quilt the checked area of the inside only. Follow the lines of the checked fabric to make quilting easier. Use matching thread.

8 Divide the strap on one side into 3 sections by stitching across it. Pin the strap ends centrally to the outside edges of the inside.

9 Ties: Cut a piece of the spotted fabric 28 × 1½in (71 × 4cm). Fold in half lengthwise right sides facing and stitch across the ends and down the length, leaving an opening centrally in the long side. Trim the seam allowance and turn through to the right side. Slipstitch the opening to close. Press. Fold the tie in half and baste in the middle of the left-hand side of the back piece.

10 Pin and baste the inside to the back, wrong sides facing. Using a piece of chalk and a cup as a guide, round off the corners. Stitch the back and inside together working close to the edge all around, catching in the straps and ties.

11 Cut 2in (5cm)-wide strips on the bias from the green spotted fabric. Join pieces until you have sufficient to go all around the roll.

12 Finish all around the roll with bias binding.

13 Napkin: Cut a 12in (30cm) square of spotted green fabric. Turn and press a double ¼in (6mm)-wide hem on the sides. Stitch. Fold the napkin and slip under the strap. Roll up and use the ties to close the roll.

Quilt the checked area of fabric only

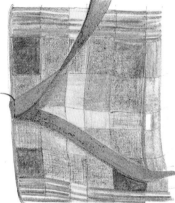

Baste the tie to the middle of the left hand side

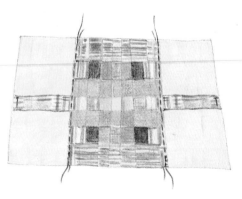

Pin the straps to the middle, topstitch the neatened checked fabric on top

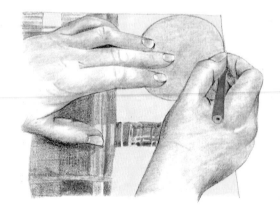

Round off the corners using a cup or glass

144

Rosettes and bows

Soft bows and rosettes on fabric streamers are a stylish way to display pictures and prints. Match the fabric to your other soft furnishings.

ROSETTES
Materials
(For 2 rosettes on streamers)
Upholstery fabric, 36 × 40in (90 × 102cm)
2 self-covering buttons, ¾in (18mm) diameter
2 curtain rings, ½in (12mm) diameter

Preparation
1 From the fabric cut 1 strip 36 × 7½in (90 × 18cm) and 1 strip 20½ × 4½in (51 × 11cm).

Making the rosette
2 Stitch the longer strip into a ring by joining the short ends. Fold in half lengthwise, raw edges together. Gather up the raw edges by hand and pull tight, forming a rosette. Fasten off the thread ends. Work the second strip in the same way.

3 Place the smaller rosette centrally on top of the larger and sew together.

4 Cover the button with fabric. Sew to the center of the rosette.

Making the streamer
5 Cut a strip of fabric 36 × 8in (90 × 20cm). Fold in half lengthwise right sides facing. Cut across one end diagonally. Stitch along the diagonal end and the long edges, leaving the short, straight end open. Trim seam allowances and turn to the right side.

6 Press with the seam to one edge. Turn in the open end and sew to the back of rosette.

7 Sew a curtain ring to the back of the rosette. The picture is hung just under the rosette and over the streamer.

BOW
Materials
(For 2 bows on streamers)
Furnishing fabric, 72 × 36in (180 × 90cm)
2 curtain rings, ½in (12mm) diameter

Preparation
1 From the fabric, cut a strip 10 × 23in (25 × 58cm).

Making the bow
2 Fold in half lengthwise right sides facing and stitch the edges together leaving an opening centrally in the long side. Trim the seam allowances and turn to the right side. Close the open seam with slipstitches.

3 Cut the center band 5½ × 4¾in (14 × 12cm). Fold in half lengthwise, stitch the long edges. Trim the seam allowances and turn to the right side.

4 Form the bow, pleating the center. Cover with the center band and sew at the back of the bow. Make the streamers in the same way as for the rosette streamer (stages 5 and 6). Sew the bows to the streamers and add a curtain ring at the back for hanging.

Cover the button with fabric

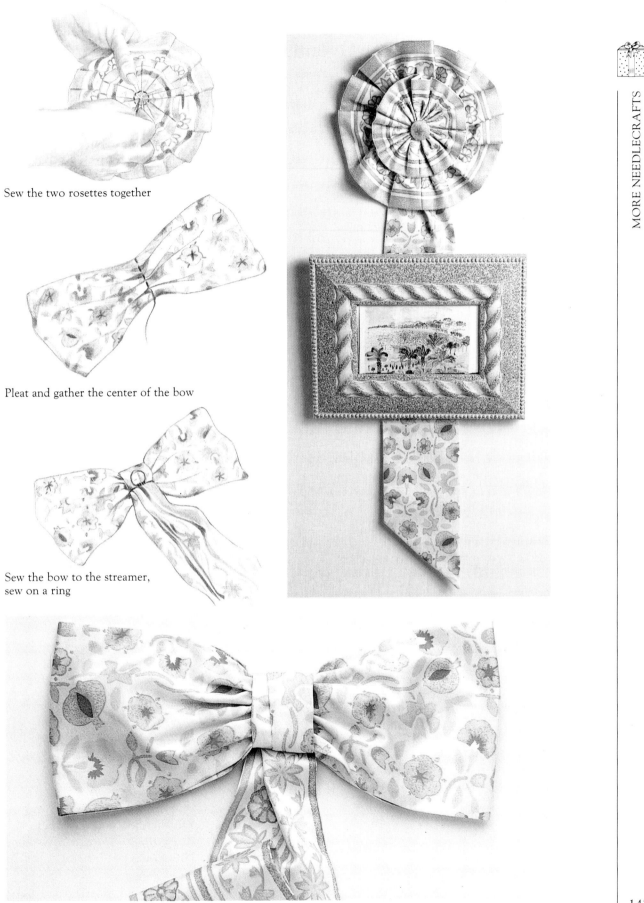

Sew the two rosettes together

Pleat and gather the center of the bow

Sew the bow to the streamer,
sew on a ring

Overnight guest

The perfect gift for the traveler – a comfortable pair of slip-ons in their own drawstring bag. Almost flat, the bag and slip-ons are easy to pack and take up hardly any space.

Materials
Floral fabric, 30 × 18in (75 × 46cm)
Thick cardboard, 12 × 10in (30 × 25cm)
Craft-weight interfacing, 12 × 10in
   (30 × 25cm)
Bias binding, ½in (12mm) wide, 2¼yd
   (2.10m) long
Lace edging, ¾in (18mm) wide, 1yd (90cm)
Cord, 1yd (90cm)

Preparation
1 Draw around a foot on a piece of stiff card. Repeat for the other foot. Cut out the 2 shapes.

2 Using the cardboard shapes as templates cut 2 shapes from interfacing and 2 from fabric for each slip-on adding ¼in (6mm) all around to each shape.

Making the slip-ons
(Make two in the same way)
3 Sandwich the cardboard between the 2 pieces of interfacing then between the 2 pieces of fabric. Baste, then stitch all around to hold the layers together.

4 For the cross-over straps, cut 2 pieces of fabric each 16 × 2in (40 × 5cm). Press the strips in half lengthwise. Baste lace along the raw edges, bind to neaten with bias binding.

5 Place the foot on the sole and place the straps over the foot in a cross, to fit. Pin together. Cut the strap ends diagonally to match the sole. Pin. Bind around the outer edges of the sole, catching in the strap ends.

Making the bag
6 For the bag cut a piece of fabric measuring 14 × 13½in (36 × 34cm). Fold in

Cut the strap diagonally to match the sole

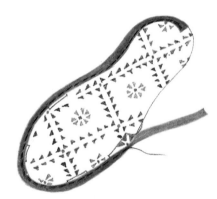

Bind around the sole, catching in the straps

half right sides facing. Pin and stitch across the base and up the side edges, leaving a ⅜in (9mm) opening 1in (2.5cm) from the top edge.

7 Turn a ¼in (6mm) hem then a ¾in (18mm) hem to form a casing. Pin and stitch all around, just above the fold of the ¼in (6mm) hem. Thread the cord through the casing, knot the ends.

8 Tuck the slip-ons into the bag.

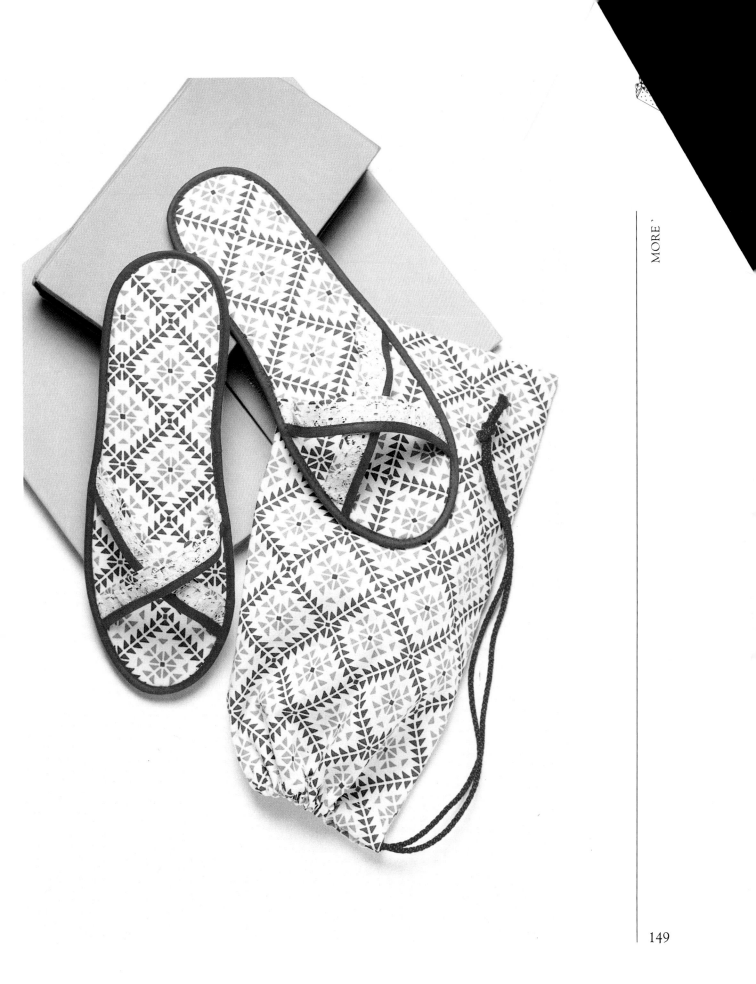

Sew easy

Sewing baskets make a wonderful gift for both young and older needleworkers. Inside this covered basket there is a pin cushion and needlecase. If you are making it for a gift, why not add a pair of scissors and a tape measure?

Materials
Basket, 5in (13cm) high, 9in (23cm) in
   diameter at the top, 7in (18cm) in
   diameter at the base
Printed cotton fabric 36in (90cm) square
Ribbon, $\frac{1}{4}$in (6mm) wide, 2yd (1.80cm)
Shirring elastic, 30in (75cm)
Elastic, 1$\frac{1}{2}$yd (1.40cm)
Heavyweight interfacing, 10in (25cm)
   square
Washable polyester toy filling
Dark blue felt, 12in (30cm) square
5 small ribbon roses
Soft embroidery thread

BASKET

1 Cut 2 pieces of fabric each 15$\frac{1}{4}$ × 7$\frac{1}{4}$in
(38 × 16cm) for the basket's lining. Cut 1
piece for the pockets, 36 × 5in
(90 × 12.5cm). For the basket base, cut 2
circles to the size of the base plus $\frac{5}{8}$in
(15mm) all around. Cut 1 base circle from
the interfacing.

2 For the basket cover, cut 2 pieces of
fabric each 18 × 10$\frac{1}{2}$in (45 × 26cm).

3 Pockets: Stitch a $\frac{1}{4}$in (6mm) hem along
the top long edge. Insert shirring elastic,
secure at each end. Do not draw up.

4 Measure and mark the strip into 6 equal
sections for 6 pockets. Measure and mark
one of the lining pieces in the same way.
Matching the bottom edges, stitch the
pocket piece to the lining down the marked
lines.

5 Fold the lining in half, right sides facing,
and stitch the short edges together,
catching in the ends of elastic.

6 Stitch the short sides of the second lining
piece, right sides facing.

7 Baste the 2 lining pieces together, right
sides facing, around the top edge. Turn
right side out. Press. Topstitch around, $\frac{3}{8}$in
(9mm) from the edge for a casing.

8 Gather up the bottom edges together.

9 Sandwich the interfacing between the
two base circles. Baste together. Turn the
lining inside out. Baste the lining to the
basket base, adjusting the gathers to fit.

10 Stitch the lining to the base. Neaten the
raw edges with zig-zag machine-stitching.
Turn the completed basket lining right side
out.

11 Basket cover: Stitch the 2 pieces of
fabric together on the short ends, right
sides facing. Press seams open. Turn to
right side.

12 Fold the ring of fabric double, almost
in half, so that $\frac{3}{8}$in (9mm) hangs longer at
the outside (this is for hem neatening later).

13 Pin, baste and stitch a $\frac{3}{8}$in (9mm)-wide
casing around the top, 1in (2.5cm) down
from the top edge.

14 Now turn the extra ⅜in (9mm) over to make a narrow double hem around the bottom edges. Make a casing, as you did for the top edge.

15 Unpick a few stitches of the side seams over the top casing. Cut the ribbon in half. Thread the ribbons through the casing. Overlap and sew the ends.

16 Unpick a few stitches on the inside of the bottom casing. Cut a 26in (66cm) length of elastic, thread through the casing. Overlap the ends, sew to join, sew up casing.

Stitch the pocket piece down the marked lines

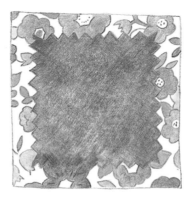

Topstitch the felt to the top fabric piece

Make an embroidery thread loop fastening on the back edge of the case

PIN CUSHION
17 Cut 2 pieces of fabric 6in (15cm) square. Cut a piece of felt, with pinking shears, 3in (7.5cm) square.

18 Topstitch the felt to the right side of one fabric piece.

19 Stitch the fabric squares together, right sides facing, leaving an opening in one side. Turn right side out, fill firmly. Close the opening with slipstitches. Decorate with 2 small ribbon roses.

NEEDLECASE
20 Cut 2 pieces of fabric each 10 × 6in (25 × 15cm). Cut a piece of heavyweight interfacing to the same size. Baste the interfacing to the wrong side of one fabric piece. Place the fabric pieces together with right sides facing. Stitch all around leaving an opening in one side. Trim seam allowances. Turn to the right side. Close the opening with slipstitches. Press.

21 Using pinking shears, cut 2 pieces of felt 7½ × 3½in (19 × 9cm). Center them on the open needlecase. Using embroidery thread, take a large stitch through the center from the outside and tie the ends together in a bow on the spine.

22 Sew a small loop of embroidery thread to the back of the case for a fastening. Sew a ribbon rose to the top. Sew another rose to the front as a button.

Cuddle and squeak

Your baby will enjoy mealtimes all the more with this happy bear bib, because the bear squeaks when its nose is pressed.

Materials
Washcloth 12in (30cm) square
Striped cotton fabric, 20 × 14in (50 × 36cm)
A flat squeaker
White bias binding, ½in (12mm) wide, 2yd
  (1.90m)
Assorted toweling in a contrast color
Black color-fast cotton fabric, for features.

Preparation
1 From the graph pattern, draw the bib
pattern on squared paper (scale 1 sq = 1in
(2.5cm)). Trace the bear's face and ears.

2 Cut the bib shape twice, on the fold,
from the striped fabric. Cut the bear's face
and outer ears from the washcloth. Cut the
inner ears from the toweling assortment.
Cut the nose and 2 eyes from the black
fabric.

Making up the bib
3 Baste the bear face, the outer ears and
the inner ears on to one bib piece. Pin and
baste. Work machine satin stitch around
inner and outer ears and then around the
face.

4 Pin and baste the eyes and nose on the
face. Work machine satin stitch all around,
adding a curved mouth under the nose.

5 Place the bibs together and mark the
position of the squeaker behind the nose
on the back bib piece. Cut a 3in (7.5cm)
square of striped fabric and stitch to the
back bib to contain the squeaker, leaving
one side open. Insert the squeaker and
complete the stitching.

6 Baste the bibs together with the squeaker
in between. Stitch all around. Bind around
all the outer edges with bias binding,
stitching with zig-zag stitches.

7 Bind around the neck edge in the same
way, but leave 9½in (24cm) lengths of
binding on each side for ties. Continue the
stitching up the ties, tucking in the raw
ends to neaten.

Graph pattern for the bib. Scale 1 sq = 1in (2.5cm)

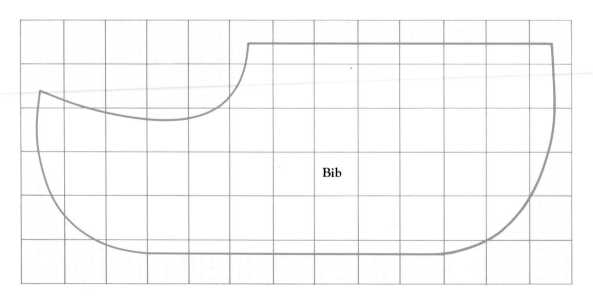

Bib

Trace the bear's face and ear from
these full-sized diagrams

Pretty and practical

Add a touch of glamor to your dressing table with quilted accessories. Display your brooch collection on an attractive cushion, conceal a tissue box under a pretty cover and make a fabric tray to hold all your odds and ends.

Materials

Cotton print fabric, 35 × 20in (89 × 50cm)
Pre-gathered lace edging, ⅝in (15mm) wide, 4yd (3.70m)
Quilted padding 30 × 16in (75 × 40cm)
Blue ribbon, ¼in (6mm) wide, 1yd (90cm)
Posterboard or thin cardboard 12 × 6in (30 × 15cm)
Small amount of polyester toy filling
Old tissue box, for a pattern

BROOCH CUSHION

Preparation

1 From the print fabric cut 2 pieces, each 7¾ × 5¾in (19 × 14.5cm). Cut 2 pieces the same size from the padding. Fuse the padding to the wrong side of the fabric pieces. Quilt both pieces following the quilting lines.

Making the brooch cushion

2 Mark a rectangle 1¼in (3cm) in from the edges on one quilted piece; this will be the front. Baste and stitch lace around the front, ⅝in (15mm) from the edges, joining the ends together. Pin and topstitch lace around the marked rectangle, joining the ends together.

3 Place the second quilted piece to the front, right sides facing. Pin and stitch all around, following the previous stitching line and leaving an opening on one side. Trim the seam allowances and across the corners. Turn right side out. Stuff firmly. Turn in the opening edges and slipstitch together.

4 Tie a small blue ribbon bow and sew to one corner.

TRAY

Preparation

5 Cut 2 pieces of fabric each measuring 11½ × 10in (29 × 25cm). Cut 2 pieces of padding to match. Fuse the padding to the wrong side of the fabric pieces. Quilt in the same way as for brooch cushion.

Making the tray

6 Pin and stitch lace to the right side of one quilted piece, ⅝in (15mm) from the edges joining the ends together to fit. Place the quilted pieces together with right sides facing. Stitch all around, following previous stitching line, and leaving one short side open. Trim corners and seam allowances. Turn right side out.

The instructions for the tray could be adapted to make a larger tray divided into 4 sections. Cut the fabrics both longer and wider and cut the posterboard stiffeners to about 2in (5cm) wide for deeper sides. Cut 2 pieces of posterboard to half the width of the tray by the depth and 2 pieces to half the length of the tray by the depth. Cover the pieces with medium-weight interfacing. For each piece of posterboard cut a piece of fabric to the actual size and another piece ¼in (6mm) larger all around. Baste the smaller piece of fabric to the posterboard, matching edges, then apply the larger piece to the other side, turning in the edges and hemming all round. Catch the dividers to the inside tray and in the middle.

Slip the stiffeners in and pin against the seam

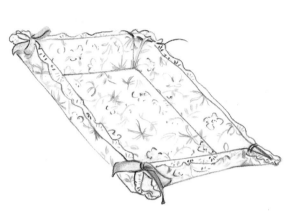

Hold the tray sides together with 2 or 3 stitches at the corners

7 From posterboard, cut 2 pieces $5\frac{1}{2} \times 1\frac{1}{2}$in (14 × 4cm) for stiffening the short sides, 2 pieces $7 \times 1\frac{1}{2}$in (18 × 4cm) for the long sides and 1 piece $7 \times 5\frac{1}{2}$in (18 × 14cm) for the base.

8 Slide one short side stiffener inside the fabric and pin centrally against the opposite seam. Slide in both long side stiffeners and pin centrally against the long sides. Slide in the base stiffener and pin to hold in position, $\frac{1}{8}$in (3mm) from the side stiffeners. Stitch around the base in the $\frac{1}{8}$in (3mm) gap, to hold the stiffeners in place. Finally slide in the remaining side stiffeners. Turn in open side seam allowance and slipstitch.

9 Fold up the tray sides and hold together with 2 or 3 stitches at each corner. Tie small blue ribbon bows. Sew a bow to each corner.

TISSUE BOX COVER
Preparation
10 Cut a piece of fabric 16in (40cm) square. Cut a piece of padding to match and fuse to the wrong side of the fabric. Quilt, as before.

11 Use the old tissue box as a pattern. Cut away the bottom. Cut up the sides to the top. Spread the box flat. Pencil around the outline of the box and the oval opening.

Remove the box pattern and mark a $\frac{5}{8}$in (15mm) seam allowance all around the outer edge. Cut out.

Making the cover
12 Cut out the oval hole, cutting $\frac{1}{2}$in (12mm) within the pencilled oval. Pin and baste lace round the pencilled oval, joining the ends together to fit. Cut a 1in (2.5cm)-wide strip of fabric on the bias, long enough to go around the opening. Bind around the oval.

13 Match the side edges, right sides facing. Stitch. Neaten and press the seams open. Turn a double $\frac{1}{4}$in (6mm) hem all around the bottom edge. Stitch. Pin and topstitch 2 rows of lace around the bottom edge of the cover, so that they overlap. Join the lace ends to fit.

14 Tie a small blue ribbon bow and sew to one side of the opening.

Interfacing fabrics
The padding material not only helps you to quilt fabric but also gives it a firmer feel which is ideal for making tissue box covers and trays. If you prefer not to quilt the fabric, use heavy-weight non-woven interfacing to back the fabric, basting it to the wrong side before making up the item.

Kitchen capers

Make a collection of pretty and practical accessories for the kitchen, mixing and matching florals and stripes.

Materials
Striped fabric, 1¾yd × 54in (1.60 × 137cm)
Floral fabric, 18 × 36in (46 × 90cm)
Medium-weight washable polyester batting,
   36 × 20in (90 × 50cm)
Curtain interlining, 33 × 6in (84 × 15cm)

TEA COZY
Preparation
1 On squared paper, draw a pattern from the graph pattern. Cut 4 shapes from striped fabric (2 for the lining) and 2 pieces from batting.

Making the cozy

2 Place a piece of batting to the wrong side of a main fabric piece, place the lining on top. Stitch the lower edge. Turn the lining to the inside. Work both sides of the cozy in the same way.

3 Make up a 2½in (6cm) length of rouleau in floral fabric for loop (see Better Techniques) and place one end at the center top of one cozy piece. Place cozy pieces together with wrong sides facing. Stitch around the curved edges.

4 From the floral fabric, cut a 1½in (4cm)-wide bias strip for binding the tea cozy. Apply the bias binding catching in the other end of the loop.

EGG COZIES
Preparation

5 Draw the shape from the graph pattern, then cut 4 pieces of fabric, 2 from the floral for the main cozy, 2 from striped lining. Cut 2 pieces from batting.

Making the cozies

6 Place the main cozy and lining pieces together, wrong sides facing, with the batting in between. Cut bias strips from the striped fabric and bind the bottom edges as before.

7 Place 2 cozy pieces together and make up a 2in (5cm) length of striped rouleau for the top loop. Baste to the top of the cozy and bind the edges (as for tea cozy) using striped fabric bias strips.

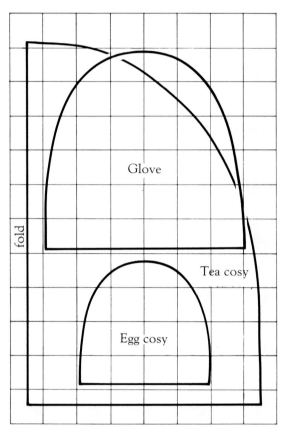

Draw the patterns for the tea cozy, egg cozy and oven glove on squared paper (scale 1 sq = 1in (2.5cm)

APRON
Preparation

8 On tracing paper, draw the half apron pattern. Fold the striped fabric in half and place the pattern to the fold. Cut out.

9 For the neck strap, cut a piece of floral fabric 20 × 1¾in (50 × 4.5cm). Fold in half lengthwise wrong sides facing. Stitch the long edges, turn to the right side.

10 For ties, cut 2 pieces each 20 × ⅝in (50cm × 15mm) from floral fabric. Fold

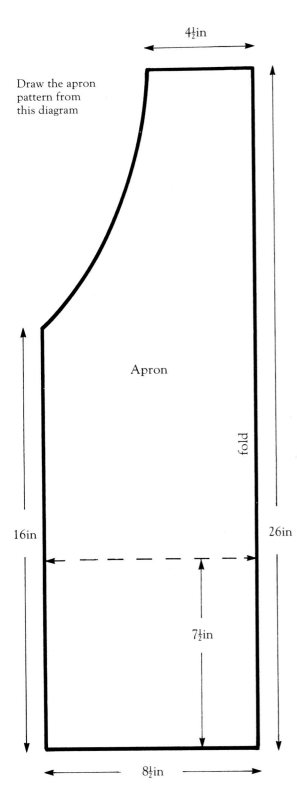

4½in

Draw the apron
pattern from
this diagram

Apron

fold

16in

26in

7½in

8½in

Making the apron

12 Turn under ⅝in (15mm) then 1in (2.5cm) on the top edges of the apron bib. Press and baste. Turn a double hem ¼in (6mm) along the armhole and side edges. Stitch. Stitch on the ties and neck strap. Bind along the top edge of the pocket with floral fabric. Press a ¼in (6mm) hem to the wrong side on the other pocket edges. Align the pocket with the bottom edge of the apron, matching the side edges, wrong side to right side of apron. Baste then stitch down the sides and across the bottom then lengthwise into 4 equal divisions.

OVEN GLOVES
Preparation

13 On squared paper, draw a pattern for the glove section. Using the pattern, cut 2 pieces from striped fabric, 2 from floral fabric and 2 from batting. From both striped fabric and batting cut 2 pieces 32¼ × 6in (82 × 15cm). Place the glove pattern on the ends, mark around and cut out.

14 Baste the batting to one piece of striped fabric. Quilt the entire oven glove with straight lines from end to end, spacing them ¾in (18mm) apart. Cut a piece of interlining to the shape of the oven glove, place on the batting. Put the second fabric piece on top, right side out.

15 Working with the glove pieces, sandwich batting between the fabrics and baste all around. Bind along the straight edges with striped fabric.

16 Hanging loop: Cut a strip of floral fabric 5 × 1½in (12.5 × 4cm). Fold in half lengthwise right sides facing. Stitch the long edges. Turn to the right side. Fold to make a hanging loop.

17 Place the glove pieces to the non-quilted side of the main oven glove section. Baste. Baste the hanging loop in the middle of one long side. Bind all around the complete oven gloves with bias-cut floral fabric strips.

each strap in half lengthwise wrong sides facing and stitch the long edges. Turn to the right side.

11 Using the pattern, cut a pocket from striped fabric.

Merry Christmas

Almost everyone loves a stocking that they can hang up at Christmas. The anticipation and excitement of prettily wrapped little gifts is all part of the joy. This festive-looking stocking will be treasured from year to year – and becomes part of the house decorations as well.

Materials
Red Christmas print fabric, 36 × 24in (90 × 60cm)
Green and white Christmas print fabric, 20 × 8in (50 × 20cm), for the cuff
Lightweight polyester batting, 36 × 30in (90 × 76cm)
Green and red felt, 6in (15cm) squares
Gold ribbon, $\frac{1}{8}$in (3mm) wide, $6\frac{1}{4}$yd (6m)
Self-adhesive plastic
Double-edged lace, 1in (2.5cm) wide, 40in (1m)
Gold-edge white satin ribbon, $\frac{3}{8}$in (9mm) wide, 40in (1m)
Green satin ribbon, $\frac{1}{8}$in (3mm) wide, $2\frac{1}{2}$yd (2m)

Preparation
1 On graph paper, draw the pattern from the graph pattern (scale: 1 sq = 1in (2.5cm)). Use the pattern to cut 4 stocking shapes from the red Christmas fabric (2 for the lining). Cut 2 stockings from batting.

Making the stocking
2 Match the batting pieces to the wrong side of the two main stocking pieces. Baste together. Pin the narrow gold ribbon in a lattice pattern over one stocking front, forming 2in (5cm) squares. Tie green ribbon bows and sew one to each intersection, catching the crossed ribbons together.

3 Baste the stocking back to the front, right sides facing. Stitch all around, leaving the top open.

4 Baste and stitch the 2 lining stockings together, leaving a 6in (15cm) opening in one side seam.

5 From red fabric, cut a loop piece 8 × 1½in (20 × 4cm). Fold in half lengthwise right sides facing and stitch, taking a ¼in (6mm) seam. Turn to the right side. Press. Fold and stitch to the top edge at the back of the main stocking.

6 Cut a piece of batting half the depth of the green fabric cuff piece. Baste the batting to the upper half of the cuff on the wrong side. Pin lace over the batted part of the cuff, ¾in (18mm) from the top edge and again across the center. Pin and stitch the gold and white ribbon centrally over the lace, anchoring it in place. Baste and then stitch the cuff into a ring. Fold in half, matching the raw edges, and baste to the top of main stocking.

7 Place the lining over the main stockings, right sides facing. Baste then stitch around the top edges, catching in the loop and cuff. Turn through the opening in the lining. Slipstitch the opening closed. Push the lining down inside the stocking.

8 **Decoration:** Trace the holly leaf and berry patterns. From green felt cut 6 leaves. Pin and baste together in pairs. Stitch all around, adding a small amount of batting as you sew. Trim the seam allowance closely.

9 From red felt cut 2 berries. Work a gathering thread around the outer edges and pull up tightly around a small amount of batting to form the berry. Fasten the thread end. Stitch the leaves and berries to the cuff.

Trace the holly leaves and berry patterns

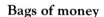

Bags of money

The Christmas stocking pattern can be adapted to make a charming and unusual Advent decoration. Have the pattern reduced by a copier so that the stocking is about 4in (10cm) long. Cut the shape from colored felt (2 pieces for each stocking) using pinking shears so that a decorative edge is obtained. Sew two shapes together. On one side brush numbers 1–24 in clear glue and, before it dries, sprinkle glitter dust on the glue. If you like, the other side of the felt stockings can have a Christmas message spelled out in glitter dust letters, such as UNTO US A CHILD IS BORN, with a star on the last stocking. Make felt hangers for each stocking, sewing them into the back edge. Small candies can be placed inside or you might decide to make

gifts of coins. Hang the stockings along a length of ribbon for a wall decoration, or fasten them to the mantle. Alternatively, they could be hung on the Christmas tree.

Deck with holly

The traceable holly leaves can be used for all kinds of Christmas fun. Cut them from cardboard and use them as templates. Use the shapes for making your own Christmas cards or for making leaf-shaped gift tags. Cut holly leaf templates from thin cardboard and stencil red and green leaves on to white kitchen paper for an inexpensive giftwrap. Make a potato printing block by cutting a leaf shape into the cut surface and show children how to print holly leaves onto cards and invitations.

Christmas Stocking

Draw the pattern for the stocking on squared paper, scale 1 sq = 1in (2.5cm)

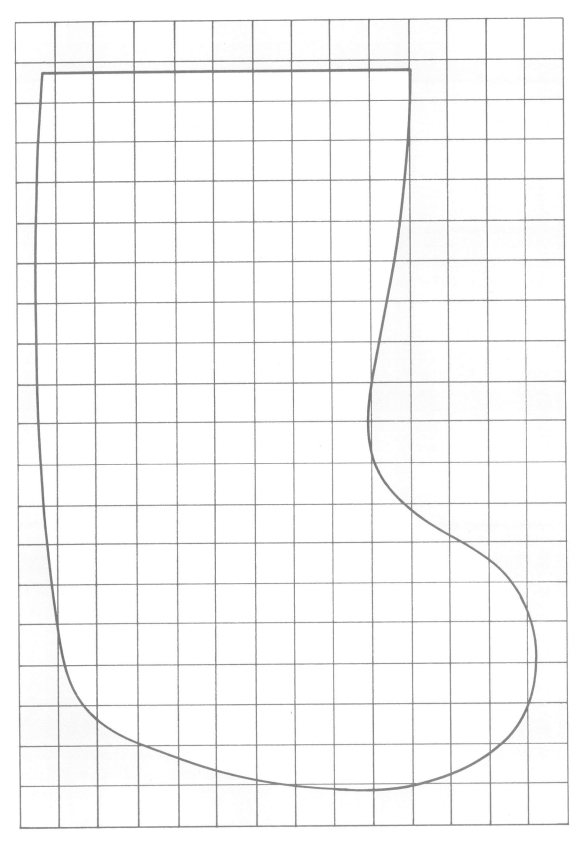

PART III

All About Paper

Stationery

Home office

Choose vibrant colors and patterns to make cheerful stationery storage. This set comprises a useful accordion file, a mini chest of drawers and a pencil holder.

ACCORDION FILE

Materials

Strong thick cardboard
Giftwrap paper laminated heavy drawing paper
Three sheets medium weight art paper (colored)
1yd (90cm) of grosgrain ribbon, 1in (2.5cm) wide
Self-adhesive plastic
Spray adhesive; clear craft glue
Masking tape

Making the file

1 From thick cardboard cut two 13 × 10in (33 × 25cm) rectangles. Cut a cardboard strip for the spine, 13 × 3¼in (33 × 8cm). Spray the laminated gift paper with adhesive on the heavy drawing paper side and cover the cardboard using the folded corner technique (page 267).

2 Cut a strip of heavy drawing paper 13 × 3in (33 × 8cm) and a strip of plastic 13 × 5in (33 × 12.5cm). Peel off the plastic backing paper and apply the heavy drawing paper centrally. Position this across the wrong side of the covered cardboard rectangles to make the spine lining.

3 Cut another strip of plastic, 16 × 4½in (41 × 11cm). Hang the folder, right side out, over the edge of the table. Gradually peel the backing paper from the plastic and stick ½in (12mm) onto the edge of the folder. Smooth over the spine. Turn the folder over and continuing to peel the backing paper, smooth the plastic onto the other edge. Fold the short ends over to the inside and press flat.

4 Ties: Cut two 18in (45cm) lengths of ribbon. Mark the position for these 1¼in

(3cm) down from the middle of the long edges on the right sides of the folder. Use a craft knife to cut slits the exact width of the ribbons. Push the ribbon ends through

Position the plastic-covered heavy drawing paper on the two cardboard rectangles

Hang the folder over the table edge, apply the self-adhesive plastic to the spine

Cover the long edges of the pleated paper with strips of self-adhesive plastic

the slits to the wrong side. Secure on the other side with a dab of clear glue and leave to dry. Cover the ribbon ends with masking tape.

5 Linings: Cut two pieces of colored medium weight art paper $12\frac{3}{4} \times 9\frac{1}{2}$ (32.5 × 24cm) to line the inside covers. Spray with adhesive and press in place.

6 Accordion sides: Make the pleated sides from two strips of colored art paper, each 13 × 8½in (33 × 21.5cm). Mark into ½in (12mm) accordion pleats and fold into shape. Open the pleats and cover the long edges with 13 × 2in (33 × 5cm) plastic strips folded in half over the pleat edges. Re-press the pleats sharply.

7 Dividers: From colored art paper cut ten 12 × 6¼ (30 × 16cm) rectangles. Edge each with folded plastic strips.

8 Run a line of adhesive down the divider sides and starting 2 pleats in, position the first divider into its pleat with the top edge of the divider level with the lower edge of the sticky plastic edging on the pleat. When all ten dividers are in position, pinch the pleats tightly together and leave the folder under a weight to form its shape.

Finishing

9 To join the pleated file section to the folder, open the folder and position the pleats centrally across the spine. Run adhesive down the end of the pleats at one end of the folder section and press to the inside cover. Press firmly to stick. Repeat at the other end of folder section making sure the pleats are aligned on both inside covers. Press to stick, and leave under a weight, closed, until dry.

Spread glue on the ends of the pleated sides, press to the inside cover

MINI CHEST OF DRAWERS
Materials

Thick cardboard for the chest, medium-weight cardboard for the drawers

A sheet of wrapping paper laminated to heavy drawing paper

Self-adhesive plastic (or contrast paper) for linings

Three small handles, optional

Spray adhesive, clear craft glue, gummed paper tape

Gold paint, optional

Making the chest

1 Draw the shape from the diagram onto thick cardboard and cut out. Score along the fold lines. Fold, then join, the edges by running adhesive down the sides. Press to stick, then reinforce the joins with strips of gummed paper tape, with an overlap to the inside.

Draw the chest shape from this diagram

Measure around the chest for the paper length, add overlap. Measure the depth of chest and add overlap on front and back edges

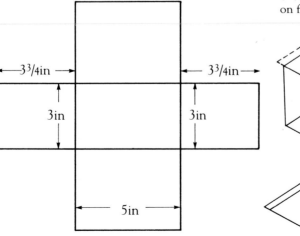

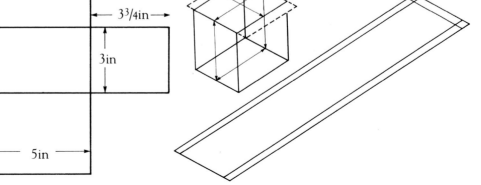

2 To make the drawer dividers measure the inside depth and width and cut two pieces of cardboard to this size. To mark the positions for these, divide the inside depth of chest into three. Run glue along the side edges of the dividers and stick in place. Reinforce the joins with strips of folded gummed tape.

3 **Covering the chest:** Measure around the top sides and base of the chest and draw a rectangle this size by the depth on wrapping paper. Add an extra $\frac{1}{2}$in (12mm) to the end for overlap. Add $\frac{3}{4}$in (18mm) to each side. Cut out. Spray the back of the paper with adhesive. Align one short edge with the base edge of the chest and smooth the paper across the base and up the side, keeping the paper straight. Continue around the chest and press the overlap to the base. Snip into the corners at the front and at each side of the drawer dividers. Smooth the overlap along the fronts of the dividers, and ease the corner and side overlaps into the chest. Neaten the corners at the back using the folded corners technique (see Better Techniques).

4 Cut strips of paper 4in (10cm) deep to fit the divider width exactly and stick across the divider edges over the overlaps and into the chest. Cut a rectangle of paper to neaten the chest back, cutting it $\frac{1}{8}$in (3mm) smaller all around then the chest measurement. Glue in place.

5 **Drawers:** Measure the inside width and depth of each drawer space and mark the shape on thin cardboard. Measure the height of the drawer space and add to the sides of the base shape. Cut out, and score along the base lines. Fold to shape. Try out the fit of the drawer in the chest, remembering that the paper cover will add bulk. Trim if necessary. Glue the edges of drawer together and reinforce with tape. Cover the drawer using the wrap around technique, extending overlaps to become linings if desired (see Better Techniques). Make 3 drawers.

6 **Handles:** Mark the center of each drawer face and pierce with a sharp tool. Insert the handle fitting (or stitch a button or bead in place with strong thread). Paint gold if required. Neaten the inside front with a length of gummed tape.

7 **Drawer linings:** Measure inside drawer sides, and cut 4 strips of lining: 2 long sides with overlaps of $\frac{1}{8}$in (3mm) at each end, and all sides with $\frac{1}{8}$in (3mm) extra depth. Stick the long linings in place first, pushing well into the corners, and aligning the top edges. Add the short side linings. Measure and cut a base piece to the exact size. Press into place to stick.

PENCIL HOLDER
Materials
Thick cardboard
Wrapping paper laminated to heavy
    drawing paper
Colored art paper for lining
Spray adhesive, clear craft glue, gummed
    paper tape

1 **Holder:** Draw a $3\frac{1}{4}$in (8cm) square for the base on cardboard. Mark $3\frac{1}{4} \times 4$in (8×10cm) rectangles on each side. Cut out and score along the base lines. Fold and glue the sides as for the chest.

2 Measure around the holder and cut paper to cover, $\frac{3}{8}$in (9mm) longer and 3in (7.5cm) deeper, to give an overlap of 2in (5cm) at the top and 1in (2.5cm) at the base. Spray the paper on the back. Align a $\frac{3}{8}$in (9mm) overlap around to one side and smooth the paper around until the end is level with the holder side. Cover the base corners using the folded corners technique. Cut a square for the outside base, $\frac{1}{8}$in (3mm) smaller than the base measurement.

3 **Lining:** Measure and cut linings for the holder in the same way as for lining the chest drawers and allowing $\frac{1}{8}$in (3mm) extra width on each side of two linings. Glue in place.

Tabletop stationery

Three different patterned papers are combined to make these elegant stationery designs. The details include contrast bindings and corner trims to add a practical touch in a very attractive way.

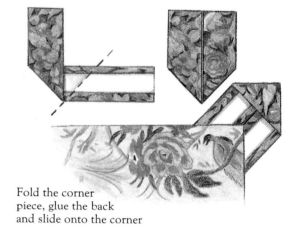

PORTFOLIO

Materials

Two coordinated giftwrap designs
Thick cardboard: two rectangles 14 × 11½in
  (35.5 × 29.5cm)
Heavy drawing paper to back main paper
Thinner (copy) paper to line contrast paper
Two sheets of art paper for linings in color
  to blend
Grosgrain ribbon for ties, 2yds (1.80m)
Hole puncher
Spray adhesive, clear craft glue, glue stick
½yd (50cm) of 2in (5cm)-wide self-adhesive
  carpet tape or
½yd (50cm) of 2–3in (5–7.5cm)-wide
  bookbinding or carpet tape

Preparation

1 Laminate the wrapping paper to the
heavy drawing paper with spray adhesive
for the main cover. Lay the laminated
paper flat, heavy drawing paper side facing

Fold the corner
piece, glue the back
and slide onto the corner

Position the glued flap to the back half of the
portfolio, aligning the crease
line ¼in (6mm) from
the outside edge

Graph pattern for the main flap and side flap (Scale 1 sq = 1in (2.5cm))

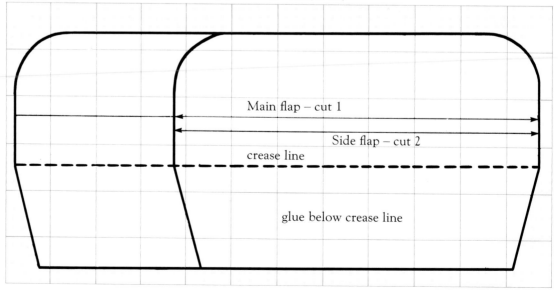

Main flap – cut 1

Side flap – cut 2

crease line

glue below crease line

and place the cardboard rectangles on this, leaving at least 2in (5cm) all around, and a 1in (2.5cm) space between the cardboards for the spine. Pencil around the cardboard shapes. Spray one side of each cardboard with adhesive, and press in position on the paper.

Making the portfolio
2 Peel the backing from the carpet or bookbinding tape, and place carefully over the position of the spine, overlapping each

piece of cardboard. Trim the tape level with the cardboard edges. Cut into the paper corners. Spread glue stick on the overlaps and press to the cardboard. Ease the paper over the spine, and use your thumb nail to ease the paper into the spine creases.

3 **Protective corners:** Cut four strips 9in (23cm) long and 3¼in (8.5cm) wide from the contrast paper. Laminate to the thin paper with spray adhesive and cut around. Mark

½in (12mm) along each long edge and gently score and fold along the line to the wrong side. Mark the center point and fold up the sides to this point. Crease sharply so that the folded edges meet. Make 4 corner pieces in the same way. The corner pieces slot in place on the portfolio. Spread clear glue on the back triangle area of each corner, slide over and press in place on the portfolio corners. Glue the remaining overlaps and press to stick, making sure the folded edges are aligned on the wrong side.

4 Ties: With the right side of the open portfolio facing, mark the center points on the tops and each side ¾in (2cm) from the edge. Cut through at these points with hole puncher using a ¼in (6mm) hole. Cut the ribbon into 6 equal lengths, and from the right side, thread the ribbon ends through the holes. Spread the ribbon end on the wrong side for 1½in (4cm) and glue flat to the cardboard with clear glue. Leave to dry.

5 Binding the spine: Cut a strip of heavy drawing paper 2¼in (6cm) by the length of the spine, plus 1in (2.5cm) on each end. Laminate to the contrast paper, allowing this to overlap by ½in (12mm) along each side. Stick excess to the wrong side with a glue stick, and cease the short ends in to fit the spine exactly. Spread clear glue along the wrong side of the strip and position over the spine. Press the overlaps to the wrong side, and smooth flat until secure. Alternatively, cover the spine with bookbinding or carpet tape.

6 Side flaps: Cut one long and two short flaps from the diagram. Crease the flaps gently along the glue line, and spread clear glue over the areas as marked. Position the flaps to the back half of the portfolio, placing each centrally and aligning the crease line ¼in (6mm) from the outside edge. Press flat and fold the flaps gently inwards.

7 Lining the portfolio: Measure the inside of the portfolio and cut a rectangle to reach right across the inside, leaving ¼in (6mm) all around, so that the lining is flush with the flap creases. Cut out. Glue the lining in place with spray adhesive and smooth flat, pressing the paper down into the spine fold. Open and close the portfolio several times to ease the lining into the spine. When dry, run a line of clear glue under the edges of the lining to secure it.

Finishing
8 Make a patchwork-style panel by mounting a square of contrast paper centrally on the front cover as shown in the picture. To do this, cut an 8in (20cm) square of thin paper and within this mark a 5½in (13cm) square. Cut this center square away to leave a frame. Glue the frame to giftwrap paper with spray adhesive, and cut around the edge leaving ½in (12mm) extra on the outer and inner edges. Turn the excess to the wrong side, and secure with glue stick. Glue the frame to the portfolio with spray adhesive.

STATIONERY BOX
The instructions given are for a flip top box to hold paper and envelops. The method is the same for any size notepaper, so you can make the box to fit your own stationery.

Materials
Cardboard
Posterboard for the inner box
Wrapping papers of two different designs
Heavy drawing paper and thin (copy) paper
Grosgrain ribbon: 5in (13cm) long and ½in (12mm) wide
Spray adhesive, glue stick, tape, brown gummed paper
Notepad and envelopes

Preparation
1 Lay the notepad and envelopes side by side, and note the measurements. On posterboard draw a rectangle to this measurement, plus ⅛in (3mm) all around. Extend 1½in (4cm) around this for the box sides and cut out. Score along the base lines and fold up the sides. Glue the sides together with clear adhesive and reinforce the joins with gummed paper tape.

Making the inner box

2 Laminate the first contrast paper to the heavy drawing paper with spray adhesive. Cover the box using the wrap around technique (see page 272), but allowing overlaps on the short sides and with the paper cut flush on the long sides. Allow sufficient top overlap to reach over to the inside base.

3 Outer box: Place the inner box on cardboard and mark around the edges. Draw around this allowing an extra ½in (12mm) on each short side and on one long side. Use a set square to check the right angles. Cut out, and then cut another identical rectangle. From cardboard cut a strip to the same length as the rectangles, and a fraction wider than the depth of the covered inner box, to make a spine. When the spine is joined to the two rectangles they should fit easily over the inner box.

179

STATIONERY

4 Place the spine strip in the center between the two rectangles and join with gummed tape stuck on both edges along the joins. Check the flexibility – the covers should lift easily on the spine.

5 Covering the outer box: Laminate the main paper to heavy drawing paper. Lay the hinged cardboard open flat on the wrong side of the giftwrap, and draw around. Mark 2in (5cm) all around the edge and cut out. Spray adhesive on the back of the wrapping paper and lay the cardboard cover over, lining up the drawn outlines. Trim the corners of the wrapping paper, cutting to the corner point at a slight angle, and press the overlaps in place. Carefully ease the paper over the spine, pressing the paper well into the fold.

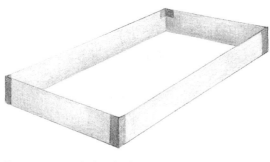

Draw a rectangle for the box tray base and extend the sides 1½in (37mm). Stick the corner joins with glue and reinforce with strips

6 Make 4 protective corners from the first contrast paper (as for the portfolio, page 176) and glue in place. Make a protective spine in the same way, but using a paper strip to fit well over each side of box spine. Use the contrast wrapping paper for this. Attach the spine to the box, smoothing the overlaps into the spine crease, and flexing the cover for easy opening.

Finishing

7 Spread clear glue over the base of the inner box, and along one long edge for the back. Press in place inside the cover, aligning so that there is an equal overlap on each side. Twist ribbon into a loop and glue the ends under the center lid with clear glue.

8 Lid lining panel: Measure the inside box, long side against the spine and the depth from the base up to within ¼in (6mm) of the lid edge. Cut a piece of heavy drawing paper to this size. Spray with adhesive and glue to the first contrast paper. Cut out, allowing ½in (12mm) extra all around for turnings. Use glue stick to secure the turnings to the wrong side. Spray the back of the lining panel with adhesive and press the lining into place. Press well into the crease of the lid fold, and ease so that the box opens easily. Run a line of clear glue around the edges of the lining and press to secure.

LETTER RACK
The rack measures 9½in (24cm) wide and 5½in (13cm) high.

Materials
Cardboard
Two sheets of giftwrap, laminated to
 cartridge paper
Clear craft glue, gummed brown paper tape
Self-adhesive velour or a piece of felt for
 the base

1 Making the rack: From cardboard, cut a rectangle 9½ × 3in (24 × 7.5cm) for the inner base. Cut the front 9½ × 2¼in (24 × 6cm), the

180

Spread glue down the back and front sections edges, press side sections in place

back 9½ × 5¼in (24 × 14cm) and the middle divider 9½ × 3¾in (24 × 9.5cm).

2 Run a line of glue along both long edges of the base and press the front and back sections to the glue. Reinforce the joins with gummed tape. Leave to dry.

3 Cut the sloping side sections. Measure the outside rack from front to back and mark this on cardboard. Draw a line from the height of the front edge to the height of the back edge. Cut out. Cut another section to match. Run a line of glue down the edges of the back and front sections, and along the edges of the base. Press side sections in place. Reinforce with gummed tape.

4 **Lining the rack:** Start by covering the inside sloping sides. Draw around the side shapes on heavy drawing paper and cut out (making sure you have a left and a right side) ¾in (18mm) longer at the top and base, and ⅛in (3mm) wider on each side. Spray paper with adhesive and press into position, pushing the paper well into corners. Pleat and press paper over to the outside at the top corners. Do not cut – smooth flat.

5 Cut paper to line the inside back. Cut to exact inside width with ¼in (6mm) extra base and ¾in (18mm) overlap at the top. Spray with adhesive and press into position.

6 Cut paper to line the inside front allowing ¼in (6mm) overlap at the base, ¾in (18mm) overlap at the front and with the side measurements to fit exactly. Glue in place. Cut a rectangle to fit inside the base exactly. Glue in place.

7 **Covering the outside:** Measure around the outside rack from the front edge around to the other front edge. Draw the shape on to the back of paper. Add ½in (12mm) overlaps on all sides, and crease inwards along the top drawn line. Stick the turnings flat with glue stick, snipping into corners as necessary. Coat the back of the paper with spray adhesive. Place the front edge overlap to the front of the rack, and smooth the paper around to the other side. Snip the base overlap to the corners, angle cut and then press to the base.

8 Measure across the front and cut paper to the exact size plus ½in (12mm) overlap at the top edge and base. Spray with adhesive and press into position. Snip the front corner to reach over to the inside.

9 **Divider:** Cut paper to twice the depth of the cardboard, and ½in (12mm) wider on each side. Cut out. Spray the back with adhesive and wrap around the cardboard. Press flat, pressing the side overlaps together. Crease these at right angles to divider. Trim the top edges of the flaps to a slight angle.

10 Pencil a mark midway between the front and back on the inside rack side. Draw a vertical line at this point. Spread glue on the outer edge of each divider flap and align with the vertical lines. Press to stick.

11 **Plinth:** Measure and cut a cardboard rectangle, ¼in (6mm) larger all around than the rack base. Cover with paper using the folded corner method (page 267) and turning the overlaps to the wrong side of the base. Neaten the underside with a piece of self-adhesive velour or felt. Spread glue evenly over the rack base and position centrally on the plinth. Press until dry.

Home Decor

Shady looks

Accordion pleats are simple to make, and ideal for shaping into lampshades, as their understated looks blend easily with most decorating styles. This shade uses a patterned wrapping paper.

The instructions are for a lampshade frame measuring 16in (40cm) at base, and 4in (10cm) at top, and about 8in (20cm) high. The paper shade which fits over is made deeper than this. The method of construction is the same whatever the frame size – follow this instructions and simply increase or decrease the length and depth of pleated paper to fit around your particular frame.

Materials
Four sheets 16 × 24 heavy drawing paper
Four sheets of wrapping paper
1¼yd (1m) narrow toning or contrasting
    cord or ribbon
Single-hole punch
Glue stick
Spray adhesive

Preparation
1 Spray one side of a sheet of heavy drawing paper with adhesive, and carefully lay a sheet of wrapping paper over. Smooth flat. Repeat with other three sheets, aligning the design motifs on each one. When dry trim papers to 14in (36cm) deep.

2 On the back of the heavy drawing paper, measure and draw out pleats as 1in (2.5cm) divisions across width. Trim the short edge of the paper to the size of the pleat if necessary. Repeat with the other sheets.

3 Making the shade: On the back of each sheet mark a line across the width 1in (2.5cm) from one long edge of the paper to mark the gathering line. Score pleats lightly along the drawn lines. Fold up into crisp accordion pleats. Join each sheet together with glue stick, overlapping the end pleats to make a long strip.

4 Turn the joined strip to the wrong side, and use a hole punch to punch holes through the folded pleats, reaching as close to the center of each pleat as possible. When complete use the punch to punch half a hole at the edge of each pleat fold, in

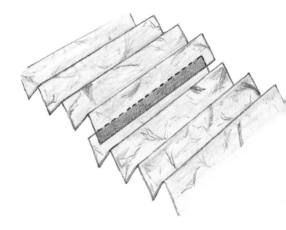

Overlap and glue the last pleat under the new paper edge to extend the length. Continue pleating

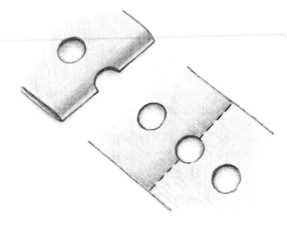

After punching holes through the middle of pleats, punch half a hole on the pleat fold

between the other holes. These edge holes will fit on to the frame top.

5 Run cord or ribbon through the holes, and check the fit of the shade around the frame. Extra pleated lengths of paper can be added at this stage if the pleats are not 'sitting well', or do not reach evenly around the frame. If the fit is good, release the cord and glue the remaining pleat ends together. Adjust the punched holes if necessary on the last joined pleats, and re-thread the cord. Tie in a double knot to secure when the shade is sitting well on the frame. Push the knots to the wrong side, or tie the ends in a decorative bow.

HOME DECOR

Frame it

The relief textures on this papier mâché picture frame are achieved with cords, paper balls and tissue paper.

Materials

Strong cardboard for frame base 10 × 8in
   (25.5 × 20.5cm)
Newspaper torn into strips, 4 × 1in
   (10 × 2.5cm)
Prepared paste with added white glue
50 Styrofoam balls, ½in (12mm) diameter
One sheet of good quality tissue paper
   larger than frame
Thick piping cord
Latex paint; enamel paints in one main
   shade and three other colors for
   sponging; clear varnish
Small pieces of sponge
Cardboard for frame backing and strut
Tissue paper in shade to match the frame
Sheet of acetate for the window
White glue and clear craft glue

Making the frame

1 Cut a 6½ × 4½in (16.5 × 11.5cm) window aperture in the center of the cardboard frame. Spread both sides of newspaper strips with paste and wrap around the cardboard frame, building up layers on the right side and keeping the back flat. After adding 3 layers leave to dry, then continue adding layers until the frame front has a slight curve. Leave to dry after every three layers. Neaten and smooth the frame back by applying strips to build the shape flat and level, with strip overlaps at the sides. Leave to dry.

2 **Adding molding:** Run a line of white glue around the edge of the window aperture and press a length of piping cord to this. Make a join at one corner, and neaten the cut ends with white glue. Check the cord is lying straight, with matching curves at the corners. Add cord to the outside edge in the same way. When dry, cover the cords with long strips of paste-

soaked newspaper, smoothing the ends to the wrong side of the frame. Leave to dry.

3 Add balls. Use white glue to secure one at each corner between the cords, and stick other balls in between, gluing them to the frame and to each other where they touch. Check alignment and leave to dry.

4 Paint a thin layer of paste over the frame, and onto one side of the tissue paper. Carefully lay the tissue paper, paste side down, over the frame. Gently tear away the tissue from the window area. Using fingers and gentle pressure, ease the tissue smoothly over the balls and into the spaces between. Press tissue around and over the frame surface, trimming and tucking the excess to the wrong side. Leave to dry.

5 **Painting the frame:** Paint latex paint on the right side of the frame. Leave to dry, then paint the wrong side. Paint the right side of the frame with 2 coats of base color enamel paint and leave to dry.

6 Pour a little of the first sponging color onto a small plate. Sponge color all over the right side of the frame. Color will adhere readily to raised areas. Leave to dry.

Draw the strut from this pattern.

Scale: 1 square = 1 sq inch (2.5cm)

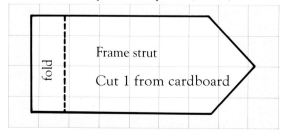

fold

Frame strut

Cut 1 from cardboard

Apply a second and third color in the same way, emphasizing selected areas with extra color. Paint the back of the frame with base color and leave to dry.

7 Frame backing: Cut a rectangle from cardboard to fit the back of the frame. Cut tissue paper to cover this, allowing an extra ½in (12mm) for turnings all around. Fix to the cardboard with spray adhesive and glue the turnings, using the folded corner method (see Better Techniques).

8 Make a strut so that the frame can be used vertically or horizontally. Cut cardboard using the pattern given as a guide. Score a fold line 1in (2.5cm) from the straight end to make a hinge. Cover the scored side with paper as before, smoothing it into the fold line and pressing the overlaps to wrong side. Cut the lining, to the same width as the strut, and the length to just above the score line. Glue in place. Place the strut on the frame back and lightly mark the position. Glue the back of the hinge and press to the backing to stick.

Finishing

9 Cut acetate slightly larger than the window aperture. Glue to the back of the frame with a little glue around the edges. Leave to dry.

10 Join the backing to the frame with a little glue run around 3 sides, leaving one side unglued to insert the picture.

Border lines

These pretty paper friezes can be used to edge shelves, pressed flat for border trims on walls – or divided into single motifs to decorate greeting cards.

Materials
Lightweight paper (copy or typing paper or
   good quality tissue paper)
Scissors with small, pointed blades
Scalpel
Stapler
Glue

Preparation
1 Trace the required pattern onto one end
of a sheet of paper, so that the pattern fold
is level with the short edge. Mark all the
areas to be cut out. Crease the paper into
accordion folds making sure the edges are
at right angles. Secure the layers by stapling
them together above and below the pattern
area.

Cutting out
2 Using a scapel, cut out the smallest areas
inside the pattern first. For accurate,
sharply defined shapes, cut from each
corner of the marked shape. Make sure the
scalpel blade pierces through all layers. Cut
out other small shapes with scissors. Cut
out the design outlines last. Discard the
excess paper and stapled areas.

Finishing
3 Continue steps 1 and 2 until you have
required length of motifs. To join strips,
either overlap the motifs to match and
secure with a little glue at the back, or trim
the motifs as necessary, and butt-join the
edges. Secure along the back with clear
cellophane tape.

4 You can iron the finished length of frieze
and mount it onto a contrasting color
paper. Cut above and below the frieze,
leaving a narrow band of contrast color to
accentuate the pattern.

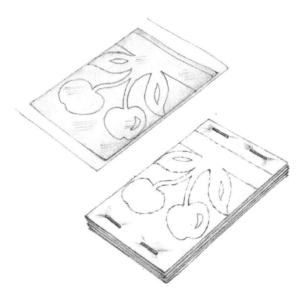

Trace the design against the short edge, accordion-fold the paper and staple

Cut from the corner of a shape using a scalpel blade

Trace these full-sized shapes for the friezes

Cherries

fold

fold

Leaves

fold

fold

All tied up

Paper ribbon comes into its own as attractive laced trims on these pretty print containers. Make them in two sizes as a matching pair, and use them to hold clutter in a decorative way!

Materials
For both containers:
Thick cardboard
Large hole punch
Spray adhesive, spray fixative (optional)
For large container:
Two sheets of wrapping paper
6yds (5.5m) paper ribbon
For small container:
One sheet of wrapping paper
3¾yds (3.5m) paper ribbon

Preparation
1 On cardboard, mark out the base shape 4½in (11cm) square and extend the lines as shown in the diagram. Cut out around the outside shape, and score along the fold lines. Fold up to shape.

Making the containers
2 To cover the container sides, lay the cardboard flat, scored side down, on the wrong side of the wrapping paper. Draw around one side, down to the base crease. Remove the cardboard. Measure a line 1½in (4cm) around the drawn outline, and cut out. Cut 3 more shapes the same and set aside. Spray the wrong side of the paper with adhesive and lay the paper sticky side up on the work surface. Press the cardboard shape onto the paper, aligning the drawn outline.

3 Carefully snip the overlaps at an angle at the base crease as shown, and fold the side overlaps to inside. Ease the base overlap gently over the crease line and glue to the base. Use the folded corner method (page 267) to neaten the overlaps on the top edge. Repeat the procedure to cover the other three sides.

4 Measure and cut a square of wrapping

paper to cover the outside of the base. It should fit exactly. Glue in place.

5 **Linings:** To make the inside linings, measure from just below the top inside edge to the base crease, then add 1in (2.5cm) for the inside base overlap. Make the lining width the same as the side measurement. Cut out 4 linings to these

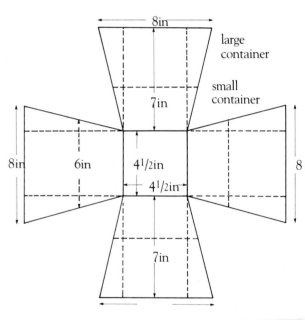

Ease the base overlap gently over the crease line, glue down

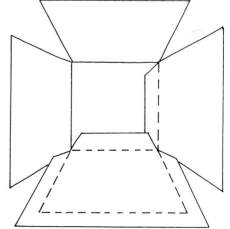

measurements from wrapping paper. Trim the edges slightly on each side so that they fit the container without going right to the cardboard edges. Spray with adhesive on the wrong side and fit in place. Ease into the crease line at the base. Trim the corners of the base overlaps as you glue them in place, to reduce bulk. Cut a square of wrapping paper to line inside the base, spray and stick in position.

Finishing

6 Large container: On one side edge, mark a dot for a hole close to the base crease, and another near the top edge. Position dots ½in (12mm) in from the side edge. Measure and mark 5 more equally spaced dots between. Mark the same positions on both edges of each side piece.

7 Small container: Mark a dot near the base and at the top of the sides, as for the large container, and position one dot in between.

8 Both containers: Resting each container side over a protective surface (a chopping board or a piece of wood), use a hole punch to punch holes at the dot positions.

9 Do not unfurl the ribbon yet. Divide and cut the ribbon into 4 equal lengths. To lace two side pieces together, thread the ribbon through opposite holes at the base, and lace up to the top. At the top edges, unfurl the ribbon ends. Lace all four sides in the same way and tie in generous bows, resting the bow knot on the top edge of the container. Trim bow ends as desired.

193

Crazy tray

Give an old tray a fresh look or personalize a new one. Crazy patchwork and the textiles of the 1920s inspired this découpage design cut from wrapping paper and colored foil.

Materials
A wood or metal tray
Selection of wrapping paper and colored
  foil protected with spray fixative
Wallpaper paste mixed full strength
Fine sandpaper, finest gauge steel wool
Clear varnish
Wax polish

Preparation
1 If you are revamping an old tray, sand down any flaky surfaces, and repaint the edges and base using an appropriate paint.

2 Trace the base shape as a pattern when cutting out the design pieces.

Working the design
3 Use a craft knife or scissors to cut a selection of larger shapes from wrapping paper, sufficient to cover the base of the tray. Overlap or butt-join the edges, but avoid overlaps of more than two layers. Be careful when placing light colors over darker patterns as they may show through. The design is worked at random as the term 'crazy' suggests, but it is a good idea to turn the tray around as you work, to vary the direction of the design.

4 Paste the back of the large paper pieces, and arrange them on the tray. Smooth away any air bubbles, and continue adding shapes and smoothing the surface as you work. Cut out foil shapes using a craft knife and straight edge, and arrange these over the wrapping paper. Continue adding shapes until you feel the design is complete.

5 Place a sheet of plain paper over the design, and press the design all over to remove any remaining air bubbles, using firm pressure with the palm of the hand. Leave work to dry completely.

Finishing
6 Apply a thin coat of varnish over the design and leave to dry in an airy place away from dust. Apply another coat of varnish, and when dry, gently rub over the surface with sandpaper. Wipe clean, and repeat with another two coats of varnish. Continue in this way, varnishing and lightly sanding until the varnish creates a smooth and perfectly even layer over the paper shapes. Ten or twelve coats of varnish should give the required effect. Finish the tray by rubbing lightly with steel wool. Finish with wax polish to shine.

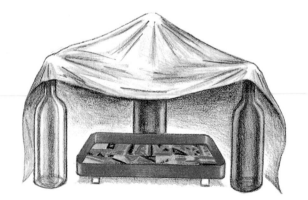

Make a 'tent' of plastic sheeting to protect the piece from dust

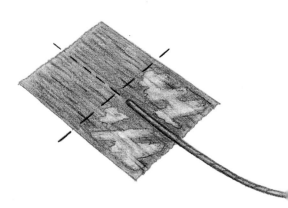

Evergreen garland

Soft woodland colors are touched with gold to create a winter garland. The understated subtle glints add a celebratory air, so the design would make an attractive Christmas decoration.

Materials
Twisted vine wreath, 10in (25cm) diameter
Gold paint (brush-on or spray)
Gold marker pen
White double crepe paper
Soft, dark green paper ribbon
Green flowermaking tape
Flower stem wires
Spool of binding wire
White pearlized flower stamens
Glue stick, clear super glue, white glue
Glitter dust
Cord to hang wreath

Preparation
1 Paint the wreath gold and leave to dry. Apply glitter by painting vine stems with white glue. Sprinkle glitter onto the glue and leave to dry. Tie a small cord loop to the back to hang the wreath.

Making the garland
2 Leaves: Trade the leaf patterns and draw onto poster board and cut out for templates. Cut 10 stem wires in half. Bind each piece with green tape. For the largest size leaf cut a 2½in (6cm) length of unravelled paper ribbon and spread glue stick on one half. Lay the binding wire on the glue centrally. Fold the paper ribbon over and press flat with hand. Fold the leaf in half along the stem. Using the largest leaf template cut around through both layers. Open the leaf flat. Color the leaf on the surface with a gold marker pen. Make 6 large leaves, 8 medium-sized leaves and 6 small leaves in the same way. You will require a shorter length of ribbon for the smaller leaves.

Fold the paper ribbon over the stem wire, fold along the wire and cut out the ivy leaves

LARGE FLOWER
Cut 3 from white double crepe paper

SMALL FLOWER
Cut 3 from white double crepe paper

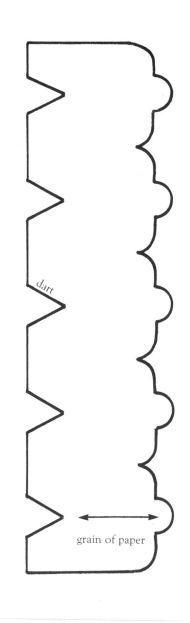

dart

← grain of paper →

Stroke gold marker pen from the petals base to the center. Glue the darts together to shape the flower

Twist 3 small leaves together, then twist in a medium-sized leaf

3 The garland is decorated with 2 sprays of leaves, each spray having 10 leaves in a mixture of the three sizes. To join the leaves into a spray, take 3 small leaves and twist the stems together. Wire-in a medium-sized leaf, then another in the same way, so that the stem gradually lengthens. Continue joining-in new leaves on each side of the stem, finishing with the largest leaves. Arrange the spray into a natural position, and set aside. Make another spray in the same way.

4 Flowers: Trace the flower patterns and make templates from posterboard. Cut 3 large and 3 small petal sections from white crepe paper. Bind a half length of stem wire with green tape. Fold 6 stamens (3 for smaller flowers) in half and bend the stem end over them to secure. Mold each petal shape by gently stretching each one sideways between thumbs. Stroke gold marker pen from base to center on each petal. When the ink is dry, spread superglue along the lower petal edge, and bring the dart edges together to shape the flower. Gather up the glued flower around the prepared stem and stamens, and press to stick. Wrap green tape around the base of the petals to secure them to the stem, and to suggest a calyx. Make the other flowers in the same way.

Finishing

5 Arrange the ivy leaves on each side of the wreath and attach the sprays with short lengths of binding wire, placed inconspicuously behind the leaves. Wire in the flowers in the same way, arranging them to mingle with the ivy leaves.

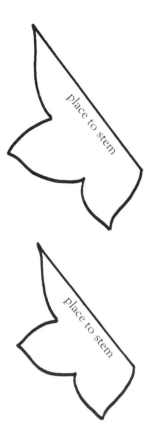

IVY LEAVES
Cut from green paper ribbon

Keep blades keen by sharpening them on a sharpening block. The blade is held at an angle and gently drawn across the surface. Sharpen first one side of the blade then turn the knife over and sharpen the other. Wipe blades with a little machine oil when they are not in use. Clean them off with a rag before a project.

Blue vase

This elegant ornament started as a plastic detergent bottle and 4 pipecleaners – but no one would guess its humble origins. Any plastic container with a pleasing shape can be used.

Materials
Plastic bottle
Newspaper torn into strips
Paper towel
Tissue paper
Mixed wallpaper paste
White glue
4 pipecleaners
White latex paint
Acrylic paints
Clear cellophane tape

Preparation
1 Cut the top from the plastic bottle.

Working the design
2 Paste newspaper strips all over the bottle, taking strips over the cut edge to the inside.

3 When the first layer is dry, work a second layer but this time using paper towel. Work 4–5 layers, alternating the paper each time. Leave to dry.

4 Cover the vase with a layer of pasted tissue.

5 Secure 2 pipecleaners, ½in (1cm) apart with strips of clear cellophane, positioning them just below the top edge of the vase. Bend the pipecleaners into shape then secure the ends to the vase with tape. Do the same on the opposite side of the vase.

6 Wrap the pipecleaner handles with strips of pasted tissue, keeping the pipecleaners ½in (1cm) apart and the curves true.

7 Apply 3 layers of pasted tissue all over the vase and leave to dry out.

8 Paint the vase inside (as far as possible) and outside with white latex paint.

9 Decorate with acrylic colors.

If the vase is to be used for fresh flowers in water, varnish both inside and out. Give 4–5 coats, leaving each coat to dry before applying the next.

Bend 2 pipecleaners to shape and tape to vase side.

Baskets for fun

Paper can be woven or braided to make decorative – and useful – baskets. Both designs can be scaled up or down in size.

WOVEN BASKET
Materials
Art paper, in 5 different colors, cut into 14
 strips 24in × 1in (61 × 2.5cm) (Cut at least
 two strips from each color)
Magazine pages, laminated to heavy
 drawing paper
Metallic cords and threads
Clear craft glue
Paper clips

Preparation
1 In weaving, the woven strips which run
vertically are called the warp, and those
which run from right to left across are
called the weft. Lay 5 warp strips of art
papers side by side, ends level, in your
chosen color sequence. Weave 5 more art
paper strips over and under these,
following the color sequence. Push the
strips tightly together, checking that the
corners are at right angles. Fold the strips
inward around the edges to mark the base
edge.

Making the basket
2 To weave the basket sides, hold the side
strips vertically and weave a new strip
through. Crease the strip at each corner to
help to hold the square shape. Push the
strips down to the base and overlap the
ends behind a vertical strip. Trim and
secure the overlaps together with glue.
Hold them with paper clips until the glue is
dry. Repeat with the other three strips.

3 **Contrast strips:** Cut the laminated
magazine pages into narrow strips, some $\frac{3}{4}$in
(18mm) wide and others $\frac{1}{2}$in (12mm) wide.
Cut some plainer color strips to the same
sizes, and some $\frac{1}{4}$in (6mm) wide.

4 Weave the contrast strips as desired
through basket weave. Secure the ends of
the strips woven around the basket sides
by overlapping and gluing as before. Secure
the vertical ends by gluing them to the
basket weave just above the top edge.

Weave the sides, creasing at the corners. Overlap
and glue the ends behind a vertical strip

For the diamond edge, fold the vertical strip, crease
and then weave into the basket side

Weave gold threads on top, or beside contrast strips. Glue the vertical thread ends to the top edge, and knot the ends of threads worked around basket. Push the knots out of sight behind the weave.

5 Diamond edging: With the outside of the basket facing, and working from left to right, start work on the first strip in from a corner. Fold a warp strip over toward you so that the strip edge is level with the edge of the top warp strip. Crease the fold, and fold the strip back to the inside of the basket to shape a triangle. Crease to shape. Weave the ends into the weave inside basket, and trim away the excess neatly. Work around the basket in this way, creasing the center of each corner triangle to shape.

6 Basket handle: Cut three 22in (56cm) strips of different colored art papers to match the basket: one ¾in (18mm) wide and two 1in (2.5cm) wide. Lay the strips one on another, and secure the layers at each end with clear glue. Lay pieces of metallic thread along the length and glue down at the ends. Wrap small lengths of contrast colored strip across the handle in the middle and halfway between the middle and the ends. Glue the strips together on the underside of the handle. Tuck one end of the handle into the side of the basket on the outside, positioning it behind the center weave on the second-from-top horizontal weave. Pull the end of the handle through the weave and check that the handle middle is centered. Adjust the handle to the required height. Tuck the end over into the top of the weave and trim excess as necessary. Repeat on other side of the handle.

BRAIDED BASKET

Materials

Three coils of 2in (5cm)-wide paper ribbon
  in three different shades
Thin, sharp sewing needle; thimble or
  leather glove
Rubber bands
Clear craft glue

Preparation

1 Unfurl the paper ribbons. Hold the ends
of 3 lengths of ribbon together (one of each
color) with rubber bands. Braid the
ribbons together keeping the tension even
so that the ribbon stays plumped and
pliable.

Making the basket

2 To start coiling, remove the rubber band
from the end of the braid and glue the ends
tightly together, keeping the braid
formation. When quite dry, cut away the
excess to leave a small neat stump. This
will be the center base of the basket.

3 Working on a flat surface, begin coiling
the braid into shape. Thread a needle with
a double thread and anchor the end under
the braid stump with a back stitch. Wear a
thimble (or leather glove) for the next stage:
keeping the braid flat, work the needle
back and forth between the sides of the
braid pulling the thread quite tightly
between the stitches to bring the braid
sides together so that the thread does not
show. Work 4 or 5 rounds for the basket
base.

4 To build the basket sides position the
braid at a slight angle to the edge of the last
base braid, and stitch to hold position.
Continue stitching around in the same way
as before to the desired depth. Finish
stitching within 6in (15cm) of your chosen
finishing point.

5 Trim the braid ends and secure with a
rubber band. Pinch the ribbon ends
together and secure with glue (as you did at
stage 2). Trim the ends neatly. Continue
stitching to the end of the braid, gradually

working-in the tapered end stump. Work
the thread ends back into the braid so that
they do not show.

Handles

6 Position these to help disguise the
finishing point. Make handles by braiding
in the same 3 colors as the basket, or make
one-color braids as a contrast. Secure the
ends as before, and braid the handle to the
required length. (Braids should be long
enough to form a deep loop without
stretching or pulling). Finish off the ends as
before, and secure with glue. Make 2
handles. Bend the handles and sew to the
inside of the basket on opposite sides. Use
matching doubled sewing thread.

Add ribbon strips by opening the end
flat, open the end of new piece, overlap
ends and glue together

Work the needle and thread back and forth
between the sides of the braid

Joining-in lengths

To join-in a length, flatten out and then
overlap the ribbon ends. Secure with
glue. Extra lengths can be added and
braided at any stage in this way, even
when the basket is being stitched to
shape. Stagger the color sequence so
that joins occur in different places.

Paper roses

Spoil yourself, or someone you love, with a bouquet of gorgeous paper blooms, or make a single rose as an impressive trim on a very special gift. Choose harmonious natural colors for a realistic look, or make fantasy roses in gold and silver for festive occasions.

Materials

Double crepe paper, in two-tone shades
(red/crimson, coral/light coral, deep
pink/light pink)
Art paper, such as tissue paper, in leaf
green
Clear glue
Flower stem wire
Spool of binding wire
Green flowermaking tape
Absorbent cotton

Preparation

1 Holding the tape diagonally to a stem
wire, wrap the tape down the stem. Bend
one end of the wire into a hook. Wrap
with a little absorbent cotton to make bud
shape, then cover with a square of crepe
paper in your chosen color. Secure the
edges of the paper down the stem with
binding wire.

Making the rose

2 Trace the petal shape and cut from
posterboard for a template. Use the
template to cut out 12 petals. With the
darkest shade of the crepe paper facing
away from you, shape each petal by gently
stretching it sideways between your
thumbs, to cup the petal shape. Then
carefully stroke the petal over a scissor
blade to curve the top edge outwards.

3 Spread glue around the inside base of
one petal and wrap it tightly around the
center 'bud' and stem. Attach each petal by
spreading glue across the base, and arrange
them opposite one another, and
overlapping until all twelve are in place.

4 Bind the bases of the petals tightly in
place with binding wire, wrapping the wire
down around the stem for a short way.
Wrap green tape over the wire and down
the stem to cover the binding wire.

5 Sepals: Trace the sepal shape and cut 5
sepals from green paper. Stretch and curl
the sepals over a scissor blade. Spread glue
on the broad end of each sepal and wrap
each one around the top of the stem,
arranging them evenly, and pressing them
to stick. Secure by wrapping green tape
around the base of the sepals, and continue
taping down the stem to end, then back up
again to top edge of tape, to thicken the
stem.

6 Leaves: Trace the leaf shapes and cut
from posterboard for templates. Use the
templates to cut from double thickness
green paper. Use the templates to cut one
large and two small leaves. Cut a stem wire
in half, and bend one piece in the middle to
a 'V'. Place the bent piece over the stem
half as shown. Bind the stems with green
tape to hold position.

7 Spread glue over one large leaf shape and
press it to the center wire. Spread glue on a
second large leaf shape and press over the
first leaf, enclosing the wire. When dry, use
small sharp scissors to make small cuts
around the edge of the leaf to suggest a
serrated outline. Repeat the process with
the smaller leaves. Attach the leaf stem to
the rose stem with green tape. Bend the
flower and leaf stems to shape them
realistically.

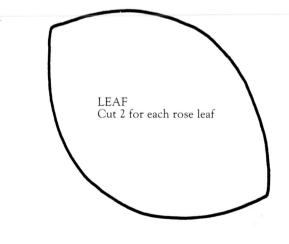

LEAF
Cut 2 for each rose leaf

LEAF
Cut 2 for each rose leaf

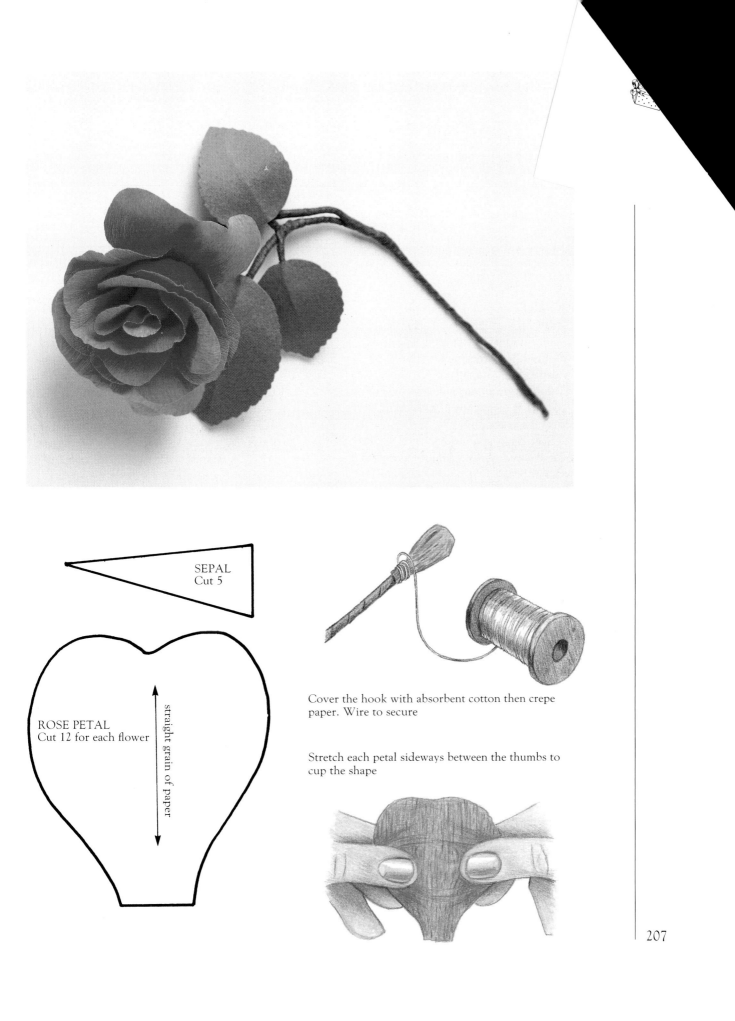

SEPAL
Cut 5

ROSE PETAL
Cut 12 for each flower

straight grain of paper

Cover the hook with absorbent cotton then crepe paper. Wire to secure

Stretch each petal sideways between the thumbs to cup the shape

Fruit bowl

Unusual bowls can be molded with wallpaper, and decorated inside and out with tissue, sparkle-textured paper and gems. Make an arrangement of fruit from papier mâché also and perhaps play a joke on your friends.

BOWL
Materials
Deep bowl with flat base for mold
Wallpaper lining paper
White glue
Fine wrapping paper: white with gold and silver flecks, purple textured
Navy blue art paper
Yellow tissue paper
Flat backed gems: black, topaz and diamonds

Preparation
1 Prepare the mold and tear the wallpaper liner into strips. Dilute the white glue to a creamy consistency with water. Work 8 layers of papier mâché over the mold. When completely dry remove the work from the mold and trim the edges level.

2 Neaten the edge of the bowl by gluing strips of lining paper over it to soften the effect. Leave to dry.

3 **Decorating the bowl:** Tear strips and patches from the other three papers and arrange and paste these as desired around the inside of the bowl. Make use of color changes and effects created by overlapping a light color such as yellow on purple and navy. Try tearing away some of the nearly dry paper to reveal color stains created on the underlying paper. Take some paper shapes over the top edge of the bowl so the design appears to flow over to the outside surface. When you are satisfied with the effect, brush over the surface with a coat of diluted white glue. Leave to dry thoroughly.

4 Decorate the outside bowl in the same way. Balance the bowl on a prop, and glue shapes in place. Brush over with diluted white glue solution and leave to dry.

5 Make a stiffer solution of white glue and use this to attach gems around the outside of the bowl (avoiding the base). When dry, repeat the process inside the bowl. Brush over all surfaces with two more coats of white glue and allow to dry thoroughly.

FUN FRUIT
Materials
Any firm fruit: apples, pears, bunch of bananas
Newspaper strips, paste with added white glue
Petroleum jelly
Craft knife and kitchen knife
White glue masking tape and fine sandpaper
Water based paints: latex paint, acrylic, watercolors or poster paints
Watercolor brushes, optional stencil brush
Varnish

Prop the upturned bowl on a jar, paste the colored paper shapes on the surface

Preparation

1 Coat the piece of fruit with petroleum jelly. Dampen the paper strips with water, then apply to the fruit. Work around the stalk pressing the paper strips well into the contours of the fruit.

Working the design

2 Build up 3 layers of paper strips using paste, then leave to dry naturally on a wire rack. (Do not dry in oven or near direct heat, as this could cause the fruit to disintegrate.) Add 3 more layers of paper strips. Allow to dry then add 2 more layers, making 8 layers altogether. Leave to dry completely.

3 Starting at the stalk of the fruit, use a craft knife to slit the papier mâché, working from stalk to base and back up to the stalk. Insert the tip of a kitchen knife into the slit and cut through the fruit. Gently scrape the fruit from each half, and clear the inside of the mold of any fruit remains. Mark each mold half with a symbol of easy matching. Repeat with the other fruit.

4 Run a line of white glue around one cut edge of the fruit shape and press to other half to join. Secure with small strips of masking tape until dry. When dry, remove the tape and reinforce the join by covering it with strips of white glue coated paper. Use more strips to cover the stalk points on the fruit, smoothing them to blend with the surface. Leave to dry. Check over the surface for any rough patches, and smooth with sandpaper if necessary.

Painting fruit
5 Prepare the fruit with a light base coat of water-based paint ready for decoration. You can try your hand at adding a colorful blush to the fruit, but if you are not entirely happy with your artistic skills, opt for plain colors – green or red apples, and bright yellow bananas – they will still look good!

6 Bananas: Paint in a basic shade of yellow. When dry, work the dark ends and greenish shading along the sides. Smudge the colors with your fingers and use a dampened brush to blend the colors naturally. Dab-on small brown 'ripe' spots at random. To re-assemble a bunch, select a few bananas which fit together well, and join them at the sides of each stalk with white glue. Hold in position until dry with masking tape. Soak a small piece of paper with white glue, and crumple it. Stick this across the stalk ends. When dry, paint it brown to match the stalks. Varnish fruit when the paint is dry.

7 Apples: Pierce a small hole in the top of the fruit. Make a stalk by tightly rolling a small strip of white glue-soaked paper. Leave to dry. Coat one end of the stalk

with white glue and push into the top of the fruit. Paint the apple an all-over shade of green or red, then work flecks and smudged stripes of shaded green or red down over the fruit. Paint the stalk and the old sepals at the base of the fruit in a brown shade. Varnish when dry.

8 Pears: Make stalks in the same way as for apples. Paint the pear an all-over shade of golden green, and smudge on touches of red or green with your fingers. Alternatively, use an almost dry stencil brush to add color and texture. Varnish when dry.

Starting at the stalk end, slit the papier mâché shell all around using a craft knife

Glue the two half apples together, then paste strips over the join

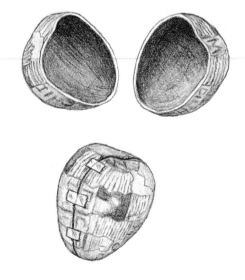

Chintz prints

These découpage candlesticks and the matching ornament are decorated with flowers cut from an antique, chintz-patterned wrapping paper. The flowers were chosen for their subtle coloring, and arranged to follow and flatter the underlying shapes.

Materials

Wooden or ceramic candlesticks, ceramic
   ornament
Wrapping paper protected with spray
   fixative
Small pair of curved nail scissors
Pair of tweezers
Wallpaper paste mixed to full strength
Multi-purpose gold paint
Finest gauge steel wool, fine sandpaper
Clear, semi-gloss varnish

Preparation

1 Cut out a selection of motifs, bearing in
mind the curves and shapes of the
candlestick and ornament which the paper
cut-outs must cover without pleating or
distorting. Choose small motifs, and
overlap them to make a larger design area
as required. Handle very small shapes with
tweezers.

2 Gently rub down wooden surfaces with
sandpaper, and wipe clean. Ceramic
surfaces should be washed to remove
surface grease, and thoroughly dried. Paint
ceramic surfaces with gold paint, and leave
to dry.

Working the design

3 Use the shape of the objects to suggest
the placing of the paper cut-outs. These
candlesticks have wide bases and molding
on the stems, giving the opportunity to
decorate these parts with plenty of pattern.
The ceramic duck has a broad, curved
back, so a garland of small flowers is built
up to emphasize this shape, while the eye
detail lends a realistic touch to the more
fanciful design.

4 Paste larger motifs to the candlesticks,
arranging duplicate shapes so they balance
evenly in the design. When decorating a
pair of candlesticks, work on both at the
same time to ensure an even distribution of
shapes. As you paste shapes in place,
smooth the surface to release any air
bubbles. Gradually add the design, turning
the object around periodically to check
that the design is well balanced. When
complete, leave to dry.

Finishing

5 Paint the object with a thin coat of
varnish and leave to dry away from dust
and direct heat. Varnish awkward shapes
which need turning over (like the duck) a
little at a time, allowing parts to dry before
continuing. Repeat with another 2 coats
and leave to dry. When dry, rub very
carefully and lightly with sand paper, and
then continue with 3 more thin layers of
varnish. Repeat sanding and varnishing
until the cut edges of the motifs can no
longer be felt with a finger. Twelve to
fourteen coats of varnish should be
sufficient. Finish the pieces by rubbing
lightly with steel wool, and then polish to a
shine with wax polish.

Cut out tiny motifs using nail scissors with curved
blades

Découpage can also be worked on the
reverse side of clear glass items. Paper
cut-outs are pasted to the inside of glass
containers or the backs of glass panels
or plates. When the paste is dry, dab
flat paint in a neutral color – cream,
beige or pale grey-green – all over the
cut-out and glass. Plates look as though
they had been hand-painted with motifs
and glass containers look like decorated
porcelain.

Jewelry

Paper beads

These beads are made from long strips of rolled paper. You can use almost any weight of paper, patterned or plain. The strips can be rolled singly, as here, or together in pairs to create two-tone effects. The metallic wrapping paper used to shape these beads makes them look like shiny enamel.

Materials
Sheet of good quality plastic foil wrapping paper
Knitting needle (the diameter smaller than the metal bead size)
Petroleum jelly
Thirty $\frac{1}{4}$in (5mm)-diameter gold metal beads
Necklace clasp
Bead stringing thread
Beading needle
Glue stick

Make two extra beads for earrings. Make them the same size or from wide paper strips as a contrast. Thread a metal bead onto a jewelry wire with a hook or eye end, and pass the wire through the paper bead. Thread on another metal bead and attach wire to earring fitting.

Preparation
1 From wrapping paper, cut 15 strips to the dimensions shown using a ruler and sharp craft knife. Taper the strips equally on each side. This ensures the bead will shape evenly when it is rolled.

2 Smear petroleum jelly on the knitting needle. Spread glue along the entire wrong side of the paper strip. Starting at the widest end, roll the strip tightly around the needle. Make sure it is rolling evenly, and adjust if necessary. Secure the end with a little more glue. Gently slide the bead off the needle.

3 Make 15 beads in the same way. Arrange them in a line, and place any beads which may look larger in the center of the line.

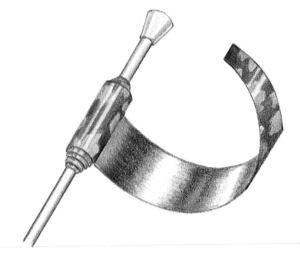

Roll the glued strip of gift paper around a knitting needle

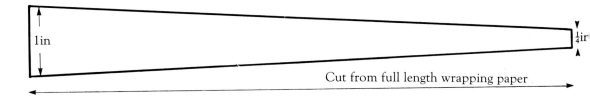

1in

$\frac{1}{4}$in

Cut from full length wrapping paper

Stringing the beads

4 Thread a beading needle with a long length of bead thread. Thread 1 metal bead, 1 paper bead, 2 metal, 1 paper, 2 metal, until the last single metal bead. Knot the thread to one half of the necklace clasp. Thread the end back down into the beads for 3in (7.5cm) and trim the end. Slide beads along the thread so that they are as close as possible. Pass the end of the thread through the other half of fastening. Knot then thread the end back into the beads for 3in (7.5cm). Trim the end.

All that glitters

Make an impressive set of fashion accessories with papier mâché, metallic paints, beads and clever touches with a gold color marker.

Materials

Cardboard tube 3¼in (8.5cm) diameter cut to 1in (2.5cm) deep
Posterboard, corrugated cardboard
Decorative upholstery nails
Paper balls 1¼in (3cm) diameter
Eighteen compressed paper balls ½in (12mm) diameter
Dark gray metallic paint; black enamel paint
Large tipped gold marker
Clear varnish, latex paint
Superglue
Jewelry components: necklace thread and clasp, brooch pin or hair clip
Twenty small gold beads for necklace
Prepared paste mixed with white glue
Glitter fabric decorating pen

1 Pewter and gold bracelet: Paste newspaper strips around the cardboard tube. Build up extra layers on the outside to curve the shape. Leave to dry.

2 Paint the bracelet with undercoat. Leave to dry. Paint the entire bracelet with metallic gray paint.

3 Follow the picture to draw curved shapes around bracelet with the gold marker pen. Color-in the drawn outlines and run gold along one edge. Leave to dry. Mark gold spots over remaining gray area and color along the other edge. Leave to dry.

4 Use pliers to trim away all but ⅜in (9mm) of six upholstery nails. Use an uncut nail to pierce a hole in the center of each gold shape. Spread superglue on the back of the trimmed nail, and push into the hole. Repeat with the other nails. When dry, coat the bracelet with varnish.

5 Earrings: Cut posterboard into two 1¼in

Pattern for large and small bows.

(3cm) squares. Cut a large compressed paper ball in half and use white glue to stick half a ball centrally on each posterboard square. When dry, turn posterboard over and use superglue to stick an earring clip to the back of each square. Leave to dry.

6 Paste very small strips of newspaper over ball and posterboard, until the front and glued clip backs are completely covered. Leave to dry.

7 Holding an earring by its clip, paint with an undercoat, and when dry, paint with gray metallic paint. When dry color-in around the square with gold, and paint gold spots on the ball. Trim a nail as for the bracelet, and attach to the center of the ball in the same way. Varnish all over. Finish the other earring to match.

8 Necklace: Use a large darning needle to pierce a hole through each paper ball, including a large ball. Paint the balls with gray metallic paint, and leave to dry (see Better Techniques). Apply a second coat and leave to dry. Decorate the balls with

gold spots. On the large ball, color-in a large gold circle around the hole. Leave to dry.

9 Add 4 upholstery nails to the large ball as for the other jewelry pieces. Varnish all the balls. Knot the thread end to half of the necklace fastening. Thread on one gold bead, a paper bead, a gold bead and so on, placing the large bead at the center. Continue threading gold beads and paper beads. Knot the thread end securely to the other necklace fastening. Pass the thread ends back down through the beads for 3in (7.5cm), trim thread ends to neaten.

1 Bow jewelry: Draw the bow shapes onto corrugated cardboard. Cut with scissors.

2 Wrap very small pasted strips over the cardboard, taking care to fold paper neatly over the points. To make the center knots, scrunch a small piece of pasted paper into a ball, and stick in position. Hold in place with small pasted strips stuck criss-cross over the top. Leave to dry. Color the fronts and backs of the bows with gold marker.

3 Bowed bracelet: Make the bracelet following stages 1–2 for the pewter and gold bangle. Color, substituting gold for gray paint.

4 Decorate the right sides of bows and bracelet using a glitter pen.

5 Use black paint and a very fine, almost dry watercolor brush to mark in shadows, and cloth fold effects (see picture). Color-in each edge of the bracelet with black. Varnish when dry.

6 Use superglue to stick a small bow to the bangle. Glue jewelry components to the backs of other bows.

Pleated jewelry

Paper can be folded accordion style and squeezed into shape to make all kinds of attractive and unusual jewelry.

Materials

Art paper in two colors
Toning wrapping paper
Spray adhesive, white glue, superglue, clear craft glue
Craft knife, straight cutting edge
Set square, small nosed pliers
Small rubber bands
You will also need:
For the earrings: Straight eye wires and earring components
For the brooch: A small hole punch, small beads with a hole diameter large enough to take narrow ribbon or cord, a brooch or lapel pin

Preparation

1 To prepare the base layer, cut a strip of art paper 3in (7.5cm) deep and about 7in (18cm) long. Mark this measurement with a set square to ensure edges are at right angles. Gently tear the paper along one long edge, so that the layered part of the tear is on the underside of the paper. From patterned wrapping paper cut a strip the same size as the base layer. Tear along one long edge in the same way. Place it over the base layer; the torn layer underneath should be visible. Tear away some more if necessary. Spray the back of the wrapping paper with adhesive and stick over the base layer. Cut the top plain layer to the same width, but to half the depth of the other layers. Tear as before, and glue in place. Trim the top and side edges through all layers if necessary. Leave to dry.

2 Pleat into accordion pleats ¼in (6mm) wide. On the right side, the first pleat should face down. If the last pleat does not face the same way as the first trim the end to match.

1 Earrings: Each earring is made from a prepared section 2½in (6cm) deep and 3½in (9cm) wide. Prepare the paper layers and pleat. Protect the pleated length with white glue by diluting white glue to a creamy consistency. Paint over the surface with a fine watercolor brush. Leave to dry. Dab a little clear glue between each pleat back and front, and press to stick. Insert a straight wire attached to an earring hook between the center pleats. Trim the straight wire if necessary to prevent it showing where pleats fan out. Apply a little superglue to the wire. Hold in place with a small rubber band around the pleats. Leave to dry.

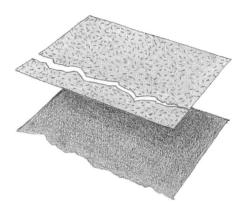

Tear the wrapping paper so that the layered edge is on the underside. Place on the torn, art paper

Pleat the three-layered piece into ¼in (6mm) accordion pleats. The first and last pleats should face down

2 Fold a narrow strip of patterned wrapping paper and glue around the pleats. Overlap at back and trim. Repeat with the other earring.

3 Brooch: Pleat a prepared strip in the same way as for the earrings, but trim the top edge so that the depth of the pleats is 1¾in (4.5cm). Trim the strip to eleven pleats. Punch a small hole through the top of each pleat, ⅛in (3mm) from the edge. Protect with white glue as for earrings. Thread a narrow ribbon through the holes, and pull up length to make an open fan shape. Thread a small bead on each side of the fan and pull the ribbon up tightly. Hold the fan closed with a rubber band

and tie a knot in the ribbon outside each bead. Thread the ribbon ends through a third bead. Remove the rubber band and tie in a knot to secure. Trim the ribbon ends level. Stick a brooch pin to the back of the fan with superglue.

By changing the colors of the papers you can create quite different effects. Try making up the designs in bright hot shades, or cool pale pastels, and you will see how versatile pleated jewelry can be.

Bright bracelets

Hand-crafted bracelets look expensive and attractive, especially when they are decorated to match an outfit. Two methods are described here – layering over a cardboard ring and over wire.

RING BRACELET
Materials
Cardboard ring
Newspaper
Paper towel
Tissue paper
Mixed wallpaper paste
White latex paint
Acrylic paints

Preparation
1 If a ready-made cardboard ring is not available, make a ring to the required dimensions.

Working the design
2 Paste torn strips of newspaper and wrap the ring. Leave to dry.

3 Paste torn strips of paper towel and wrap the ring. Leave to dry.

4 Continue wrapping the ring with alternate layers of newspaper and paper towel strips until the edges are rounded.

5 At this stage, you can finish the bracelet with 2–3 layers of pasted tissue to smooth off the surface. Alternatively, if a rounded shape is required, build up the thickness of the bracelet by applying strips around it. Finish with strips of pasted tissue.

6 Paint the finished bracelet with white latex paint then decorate.

WIRE AND TAPE BRACELET
Materials
Florists' stub wires
Masking tape
Newspaper
Mixed wallpaper paste
Tissue paper
White latex paint
Acrylic paints

Preparation
1 Form two circlets of wire, twisting the ends together. Bind with pasted tissue until the joins cannot be seen.

2 Join the two rings to make a bracelet of the desired width using masking tape.

Making card rings
Using a compass, draw a circle to the desired size on posterboard. Cut out the hole. Cut a strip of posterboard to the depth of the bracelet. Fit it into the hole. Allow the strip to expand and fill the hole and then mark the overlap. Remove the strip and trim away the excess posterboard. Butt the strip ends and tape the join. This method can also be used to make cardboard tubes.

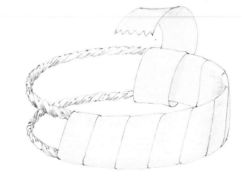

Join the two tissue-covered wire rings with strips of masking tape.

Working the design

3 Cover the bracelet with small, torn, pasted newspaper pieces until the desired thickness has been built up. Finish with 2–3 layers of pasted tissue.

4 Paint the bracelet with white latex paint inside and out.

5 Decorate the bracelet with painted designs using acrylic paints. Alternatively, choose one of the decorating techniques described.

Ideas for decorating

● Press craft gemstones into the final layers of pasted tissue to make indentations, then stick the stones in place when the papier mâché is dry.
● Draw lines of glue around the painted bracelet and press thin, gold cord along the lines.·Varnish over the cords afterwards.
● Crumple ovals of colored foil, stick in place and edge them with gold cord. Give the decoration 2 coats of varnish.

Toys and Origami

Origami boxes

Origami – the Japanese art of paper folding – has been popular for hundreds of years. These classic designs are made from a basic square of paper. You can vary the finished effect by changing the size of the square, and by working two paper squares together as a contrast. Use the boxes to present gifts and candy, or to hold small stationery items.

Materials
Pre-cut squares of Origami paper, or thin art paper or wrapping paper. (Choose any paper which takes a crease easily. Start by working on a single 10in (25cm) practice square of thin copy paper.)
Glue stick

PLEATED DIAMOND BOX
This box has a pleated diamond shaped top edge, and stands on four triangular shaped feet.

Preparation
1 Cut 2 paper squares to the required size. Place both sheets together, wrong sides facing and secure at the center with a small dab of glue. Smooth flat. Crease diagonally both ways as shown.

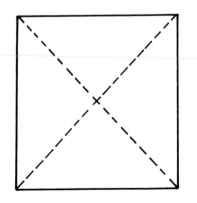

2 Fold the corners to the center.

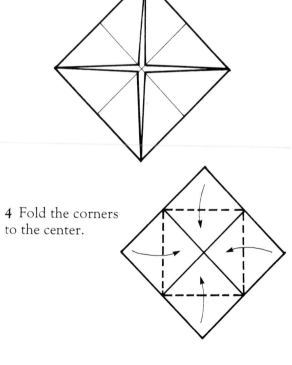

3 The paper now looks like this. Turn it over.

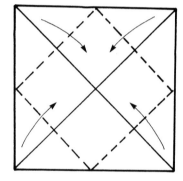

4 Fold the corners to the center.

5 Fold over the points as shown.

6 The piece now looks like this. Turn it over.

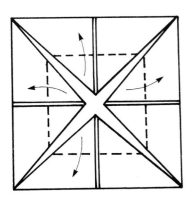

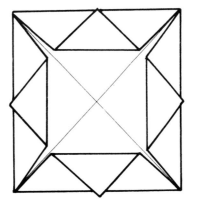

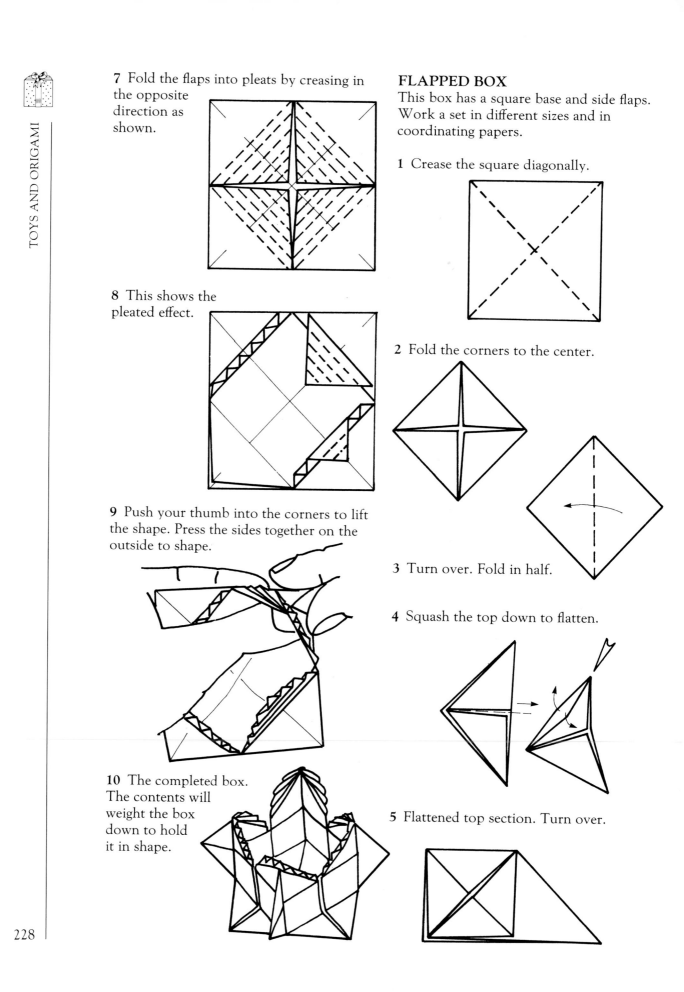

7 Fold the flaps into pleats by creasing in the opposite direction as shown.

8 This shows the pleated effect.

9 Push your thumb into the corners to lift the shape. Press the sides together on the outside to shape.

10 The completed box. The contents will weight the box down to hold it in shape.

FLAPPED BOX

This box has a square base and side flaps. Work a set in different sizes and in coordinating papers.

1 Crease the square diagonally.

2 Fold the corners to the center.

3 Turn over. Fold in half.

4 Squash the top down to flatten.

5 Flattened top section. Turn over.

6 Lift the flap up.

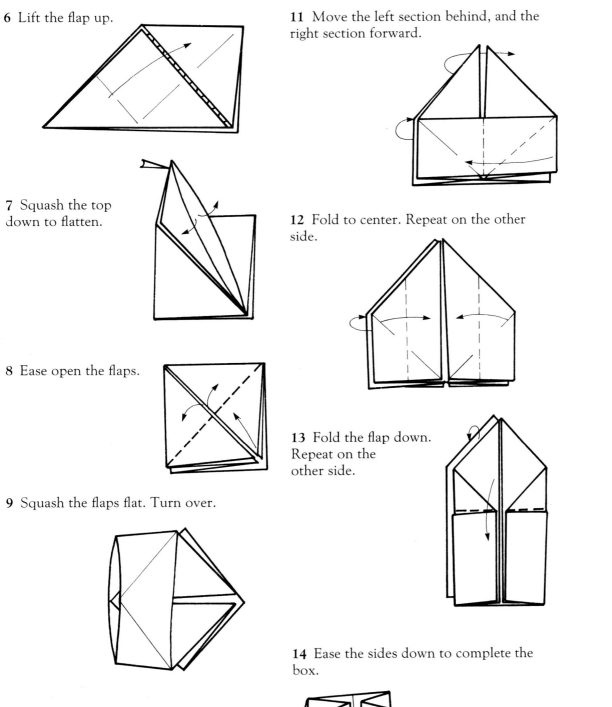

7 Squash the top down to flatten.

8 Ease open the flaps.

9 Squash the flaps flat. Turn over.

10 Repeat with the flaps on this side.

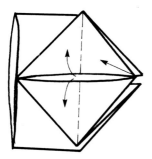

11 Move the left section behind, and the right section forward.

12 Fold to center. Repeat on the other side.

13 Fold the flap down. Repeat on the other side.

14 Ease the sides down to complete the box.

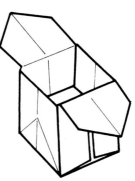

Spotty dog

Amuse your friends with this playful dog, whose appealing expression and floppy ears are sure to capture their hearts. You can make the mask complete with bone, or as a simplified version – just add a tongue.

Materials
Dressmakers' squared paper, scale
   1 sq = 1 in (2.5cm)
Thin white cardboard or posterboard
Two shades of brown art paper, dark for
   ears and chin, light for eye patch
Black paper, black sticky-back velour for
   nose
Two shades of pink art paper – dark for
   tongue, light for lip
Two shades of gray art paper, mid gray for
   bone, dark gray for upper lip/nose line
Cream paper for teeth
Hole punch
Thin round elastic
Two self adhesive pads
Spray adhesive, double sided clear
   cellophane tape

Preparation
1 Draw patterns from the graph patterns on pages 232–3. Trace to use as a guide when positioning the mask details. Transfer the mask front pattern to thin cardboard and cut out. Score lightly and fold along the tops of the ears.

2 Trace the ear shapes onto dark brown paper, cut out and glue in place, level with the fold line. Cut out the patch and stick in place. Cut out the gray lip line and glue in place.

3 Punch the muzzle spots from dark brown paper and glue in place. Cut out 2 black eye circles, and the dark brown eyebrows. Cut a nose from black velour stuck to black paper. Stick 2 adhesive pads on the back of the nose shape and stick the nose on the mask. Leave the mask at this stage if you wish, and add a tongue, glued behind the muzzle.

Mask backing
4 Transfer the mask backing pattern to white cardboard and cut out. Cut out all other shapes from paper as outlined on the pattern.

5 Using the tracing to help you place the shapes, glue the brown chin shape in place, and glue the tongue over this. Cut out the teeth and lip shapes and glue the lip over the teeth. Glue the lip in place making sure the teeth remain free.

6 Cut out the bone. Lay the bone between the teeth, and secure by placing a little double sided clear cellophane tape behind the bone.

Assembling the mask
7 Open the mask front flat, and avoiding the ears (mask these off with a spare piece of paper) spray the back with adhesive. Lay the mask over the mask backing, and ease the teeth to the front of the mask. Leave to dry.

8 Use the hole punch to cut holes for eyes and holes for the elastic. Measure the elastic to reach around the head, thread through the holes and tie in a knot at the back.

DOG MASK FRONT
Cut 1 from white posterboard/paper

1 sq = 1 inch (2.5cm)

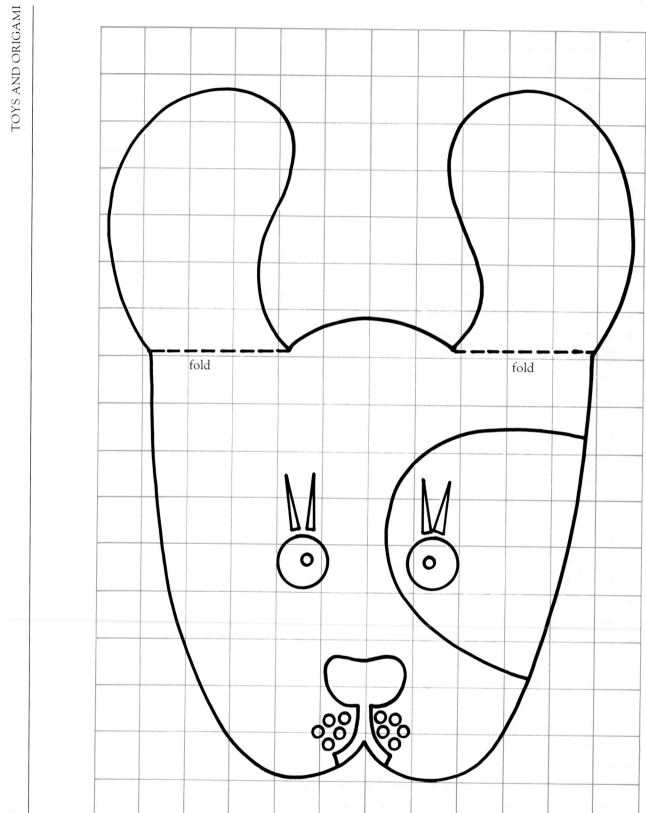

fold   fold

MASK BACKING
Cut outline shape from white
posterboard/paper

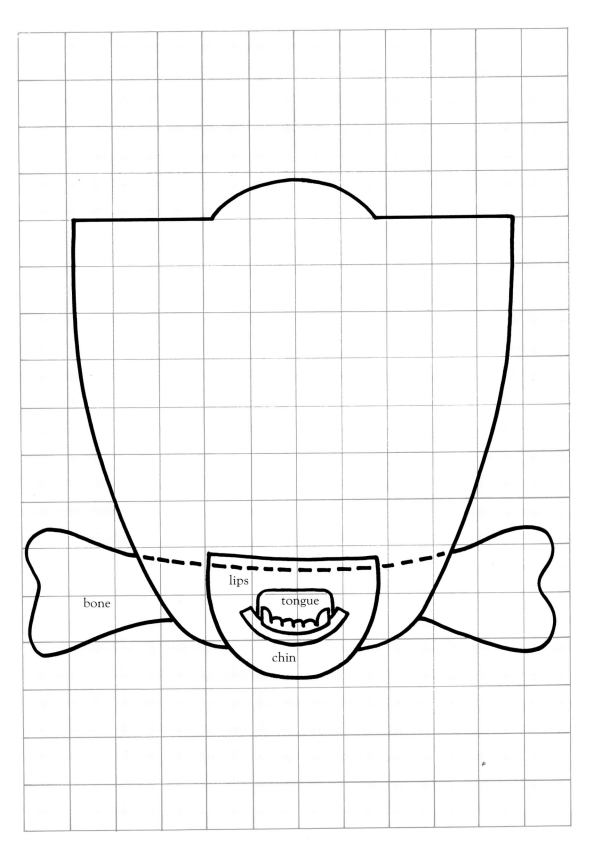

bone

lips

tongue

chin

Flower mobile

Multi-colored flowers create this easy-to-make mobile. Made from heavy drawing paper and hung from wires they are child's play!

Materials
Heavy drawing paper
Mobile wires: one 10½in (27cm) long, two
  7½in (19cm) long
Felt tipped markers (seven colors)
Glue stick
Invisible thread, sewing needle, clear
  cellophane tape

Making the flowers
1 Trace the half flower shape and retrace to make a template. Cut out 2 shapes for each flower from heavy drawing paper. Crease lightly along the fold lines and cut along one line to the center. Cut out 14 shapes (7 flowers).

2 Use felt tipped markers and refer to the picture as a guide to color the flowers with simple one-stroke marks. Color a flower center and then work around the outsides of the petals. To help balance the final effect, try to introduce a touch of all 7 colors on each flower.

3 To shape a flower, spread glue stick over the triangular section marked 'cut'. Fold the flower into shape by pressing the glued area under the adjoining triangle. To complete the flower, spread glue stick on the back of each scallop edge of one flower shape, and join to another flower shape, matching overlap points. Press together to stick, and trim the edges level to neaten if necessary.

Arrange the mobile on a large sheet of paper like this

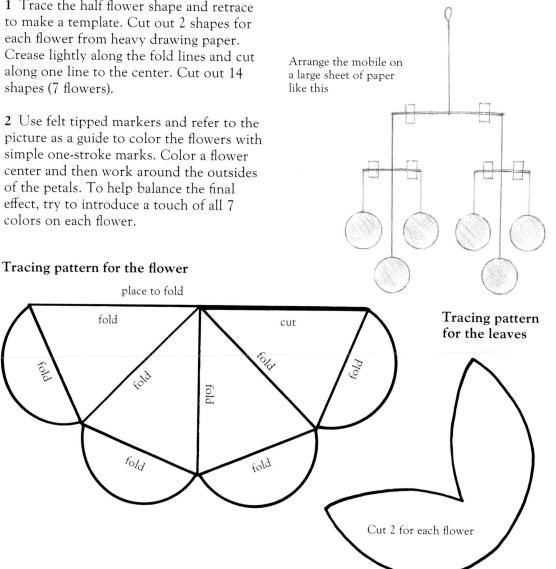

Tracing pattern for the leaves

Tracing pattern for the flower

place to fold

fold   cut

fold   fold   fold   fold   fold

fold   fold

Cut 2 for each flower

Assembling the mobile

4 Secure the largest mobile wire with clear cellophane tape to a large sheet of paper or a smooth work surface. Lay short wires about 7½in (18cm) below this, with the end points of the large wire level with the centers. Secure with clear cellophane tape. Take a length of invisible thread and securely tie a piece 15in (38cm) long to the mid-point of the large wire. Tie a loop at the other end to hang the mobile.

5 Pierce a needle through the flower scallop at the overlapping point and thread a short length of thread through this. Secure by knotting. Place a flower 3in (7.5cm) below the center of the wire. Secure the thread position with clear cellophane tape and knot the end to the wire. Join flowers to the small wires, positioning each one 3in (7.5cm) from the wire ends, securing the position with clear

cellophane tape as before. Hang a flower from the center point of each short wire, positioning each one 10in (25cm) from the center of the wire.

6 Adding leaves: Trace the leaf pattern and cut a template. Cut out 14 leaf shapes. Color one side of each. Spread glue stick on the wrong side of one leaf, and attach to the wrong side of another leaf. Check the fit of the pair and trim as necessary. Spread glue stick on the wrong side of one leaf, slip the leaf pair around the thread, just above the flower, and press leaves together to stick. Repeat with all flowers.

Hanging the mobile

7 Remove the tape clear cellophane tape carefully, and hang the mobile where it will catch the draft – under a light fixture, or near a window.

235

Greetings

Treasure bags

These little woven containers are so simple to make and are ideal for holding small gifts or candy.

Materials
Strong, colored paper, or laminate
  wrapping paper to heavy drawing paper
  for the container base
Contrast papers (prepared to equal weight)
  for weaving
Clear craft glue

1 To make the base, follow the diagram. Cut a rectangle $6\frac{1}{4} \times 3$in (16×7.5cm) from paper. Draw a line $\frac{1}{4}$in (6mm) all around inside the outline. Within this, measure and mark lines $\frac{1}{2}$in (12mm) apart. Cut along the lines with a craft knife. Fold the paper in half across its width.

2 Cut 6 strips of contrast paper, each $\frac{1}{2}$in (12mm) wide, and long enough to wrap around the bag with a generous overlap. With the base folded, weave one strip across the next to the fold line. Continue weaving across the back. Weave in the

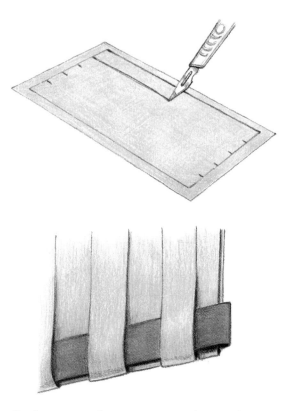

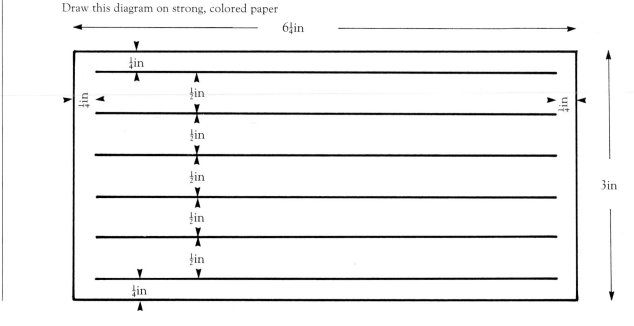

Cut long strips of contrast paper and weave them around the folded base piece

Draw this diagram on strong, colored paper

$6\frac{1}{4}$in

$\frac{1}{4}$in

$\frac{1}{4}$in

$\frac{1}{2}$in

$\frac{1}{4}$in

$\frac{1}{2}$in

$\frac{1}{2}$in

$\frac{1}{2}$in

$\frac{1}{2}$in

$\frac{1}{4}$in

3in

ends securely into the inside and outside of the bag. Trim the excess strip so that the ends do not show on the outside. Continue weaving in the same way with 4 more strips.

Handle

3 To make the handle, cut the remaining strip to 8in (20cm) long and weave each end into the pattern at the center on the insides of the bag. Secure with glue.

Surprises in store

These cone boxes are ideal for jewelry and other small special gifts. Folded to shape from one piece of posterboard, they are quick to make and a pleasure to decorate with colorful scraps and trims.

Materials
Posterboard
Wrapping paper
Spray adhesive
Clear craft glue
Decorative paper scraps or other trims
Cord for loops
Small hole punch

Making the boxes
1 Trace the full-sized pattern on pages 242–3 joining lines where indicated with arrows. Trace shape onto posterboard. Cut around the outline and crease along the fold lines. Bend the cone into shape.

2 Flatten the shape, and spray the right side with adhesive. Press onto wrapping paper, smooth flat and cut around the posterboard edges. Pierce a hole through the center of the lid. Re-crease along the fold lines to shape the box.

3 Spread glue along the side flap and press to stick. Thread a loop of cord through the hole in the lid and knot on the underside. Glue a decorative scrap or trim on the box front.

4 To fasten the lid closed, stick a little double-sided clear cellophane tape on the right side of the lid flaps. Remove the protective paper when the gift is inside, and seal by placing the flaps inside the box.

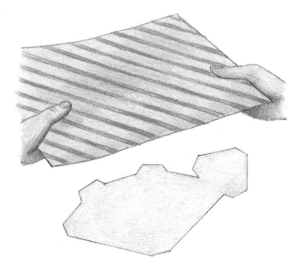

Spray the posterboard with adhesive, press on a piece of wrapping paper

Glue the side flap and form the cone. Knot a cord loop through the lid hole

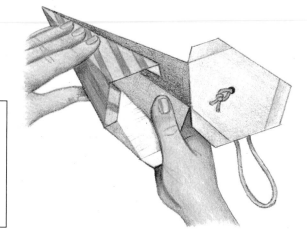

Make the boxes in seasonal colors to hang as decorations or special favors on the Christmas tree. Decorate the fronts with baubles or scraps of winter greenery and berries and fill with candy, nuts or candied fruits.

240

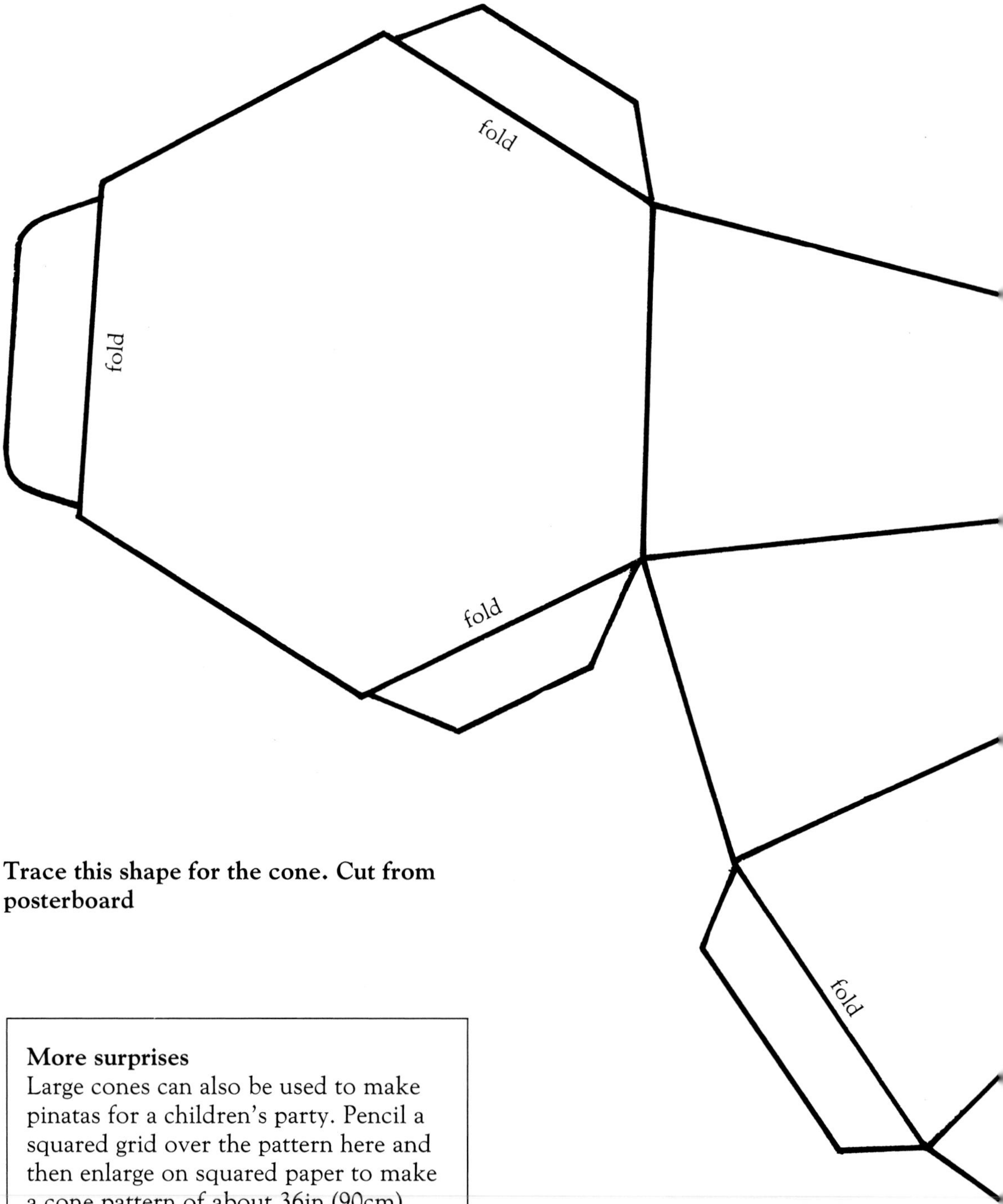

fold

fold

fold

fold

Trace this shape for the cone. Cut from posterboard

More surprises
Large cones can also be used to make pinatas for a children's party. Pencil a squared grid over the pattern here and then enlarge on squared paper to make a cone pattern of about 36in (90cm) long. Cut the cone from sheets of flexible, cardboard (you will have to tape sheets together to achieve the area required). Cover the cardboard with bright paper or paint designs over it. Fill the cone with small gifts and hang it high on the wall or over a doorway. During the party, children are given sticks and encouraged to beat the pinata until it opens and showers them with gifts.

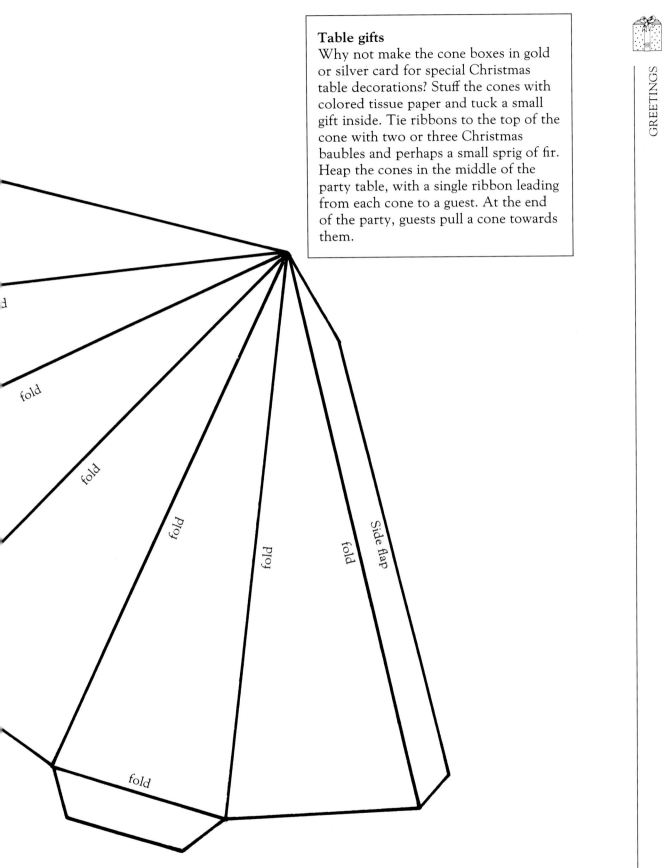

Table gifts
Why not make the cone boxes in gold
or silver card for special Christmas
table decorations? Stuff the cones with
colored tissue paper and tuck a small
gift inside. Tie ribbons to the top of the
cone with two or three Christmas
baubles and perhaps a small sprig of fir.
Heap the cones in the middle of the
party table, with a single ribbon leading
from each cone to a guest. At the end
of the party, guests pull a cone towards
them.

fold

fold

fold

fold

fold

fold

Side flap

fold

Cat and mouse

These popular pets make perfect greeting cards, and their appealing expressions are easy to achieve with the help of toymaking accessories.

Materials
For both designs:
Spray adhesive and clear craft glue
Sharp sewing needle
For the cat:
Orange art paper
White heavy drawing paper
Scrap of pink paper
Six black toy whiskers
2 cat eyes and one nose
Two self-adhesive pads
Black felt tipped marker (or black crayon)
For the mouse:
Dark gray art paper
Pink art paper
Scrap of black sticky-backed velour (or black paper)
6in (15cm) length of very narrow pale pink ribbon
Six transparent plastic whiskers
2 small goggly eyes
Scrap of white paper
One self-adhesive pad

THE CAT
Preparation
1 Trace the cat pattern on pages 246–7, joining lines where indicated with arrows. Draw a line on a sheet of orange paper, score gently and fold in half. Place the fold to the fold line on the cat tracing. Cut through both thicknesses. Trace the head separately and cut out from a single thickness of paper.

2 Trace and cut out the head and body markings from white paper. Spray the backs of the pieces with adhesive, and position on cat shape using the tracing as a guide. Cut out a pink tongue and glue in place. Draw claws on cat's paws.

3 Use a needle to pierce holes for whiskers. Insert each whisker from the back, trimming off any plastic end pieces. Arrange the whiskers so they lay flat and are evenly spaced. Secure the whiskers at the back with a scrap of orange paper glued over the whisker ends. Trim the whiskers to the desired length.

4 Glue the eyes and nose in place.

5 Using the tracing as a guide, place two adhesive pads on the body where the head overlaps, and position the head over these.

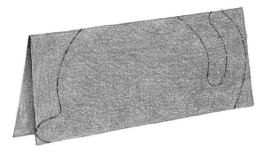

Draw the cat's body only on the folded orange paper. The head is cut separately

Secure the mouse whiskers on the wrong side with strips of glued paper

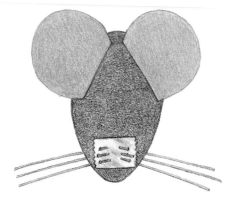

THE MOUSE

6 Follow the basic instructions for tracing the mouse pattern (pages 246–7) and cut the mouse body from folded gray paper, and head from a single layer of gray paper. Cut out pink ears and glue behind head. Cut out a pink foot, and draw claws on it. Glue in place.

7 Glue the eyes in place. Pierce the face for the whiskers and insert them. Secure the whiskers with glued paper as for the cat. Snip teeth from white paper and glue in position. Glue the nose in place.

8 Pierce a small hole for the tail, and thread ribbon through. Knot on the wrong side.

9 Place an adhesive pad on the body behind the head area, and stick the head in place.

Trace these patterns for the Cat and Mouse

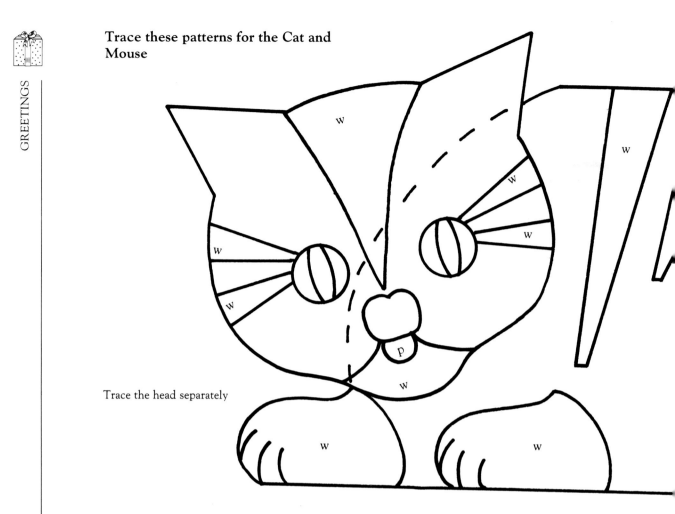

Trace the head separately

Cat calendar
The cat card can be adapted to make an amusing calendar. Construct the cat on a single piece of orange paper. Cut the same shape from orange paper twice more and mount the finished cat on double-sided adhesive pads, as described for the 3-D découpage cards on page 252. You might also lift forward the cat's head and paws in the same way. Cut a rectangle of cardboard and cover it with wrapping paper. Glue the cat to the upper half of the cardboard and a calendar block to the lower half. You can either make a strut for the back so that the calendar stands up or a ribbon hanger can be glued behind the top edge.

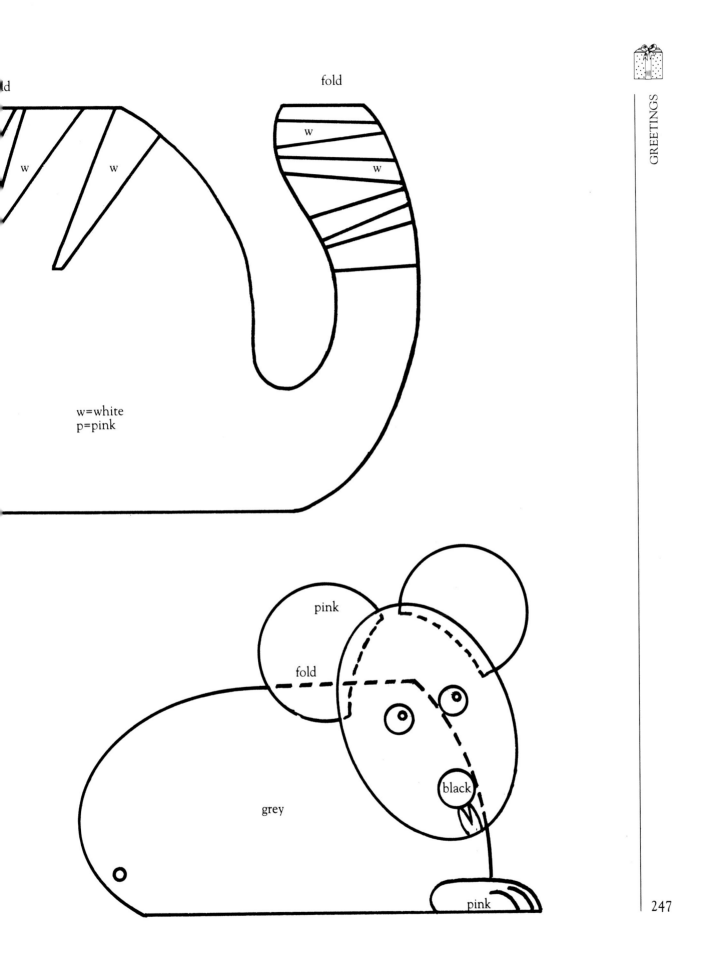

fold

fold

w

w

w

w

w=white
p=pink

pink

fold

grey

black

pink

Carried away

A gift bag is an ever popular, versatile container – the ideal solution for wrapping an awkwardly shaped gift, and attractive enough to keep as a lightweight carryall for all kinds of miscellaneous items.

Materials
Decorative wrapping paper (or patterned wallpaper)
Heavy drawing paper (or wallpaper lining paper)
Posterboard
Spray adhesive
Glue stick
Cord or ribbon for handles
String for gift tags
Hole punch

Making gift bags
A gift bag can be any size you wish to make, simply by adapting the basic pattern and following one basic rule: the depth of the base overlap sections on the bag (marked on pattern **A** plus half again) should always measure more than half the depth (marked **A**) of each side. All **A** measurements should be equal, so that the bag holds its shape well and folds flat. By simply checking these proportions you can make professional looking gift bags, from mini to maxi sizes. When making large bags, join papers at each side so that the joins do not show.

Making the lining
1 Following the diagram (on page 250), draw the bag measurements onto a sheet of heavy drawing paper. Cut out. Starting with the main vertical lines, crease the fold lines to shape. Crease the base line and the fold line which runs across the back section. Carefully crease the side triangular shaped sections. Next, fold the side lines together, and pinch the triangles into place. Open out again.

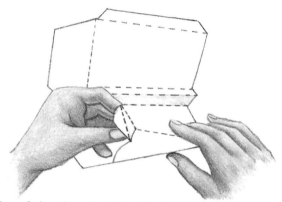

Spread glue along the right side of the side flap, press to the inside edge of the bag side

With one hand inside as a support, press the flaps together to stick

Press the base section along the crease lines

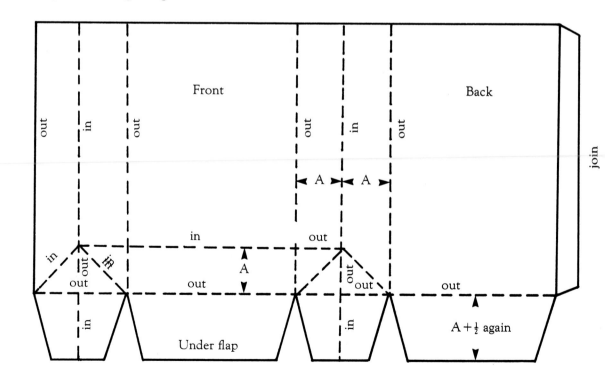

Covering the lining

2 Lay the heavy drawing paper flat, creased side facing and spray with adhesive. Lay the covering paper flat wrong side facing, and press the heavy drawing paper, sticky side down, onto this. Position it so that there is an overlap of covering paper at the top edge of about 3in (7.5cm). Smooth flat on both sides of paper. Trim level with the heavy drawing paper edges, adjusting the top overlap size accurately if necessary. Fold along the creases to shape the paper smoothly.

3 Cut a reinforcing strip of posterboard to the same depth as the overlap and as wide as the bag (excluding the side flap) and stick across the top of the heavy drawing paper. Spread glue underneath the top overlap and press flat to stick to the posterboard strip.

4 Spread glue along the right side of the side flap, and press to the inside edge of the bag side. Align the edges, and top and base lines neatly. Press to stick.

5 Turn the bag upside down. Spread glue on the edges of the right sides of the base side flaps, and along the edge of the wrong side of the under flap. With one hand inside the bag as support, press the flaps together to stick, making sure that the bag keeps its shape. Now spread glue under the remaining base flap, and press to stick.

6 Smooth the gift bag edges, making sure that they are all aligned. Gently press the base section flat along the crease lines, so that the base rests flat against the bag.

The handles

7 Position the handles to suit the proportions of the bag. The holes for the handles are marked with a hole punch. To achieve a good balance, position these between a third to a quarter of the front width in from each side. Place the holes about ¾in (18mm) down from the top edge, or as far as the punch will reach, to avoid tearing the paper.

Diagram for the gift bag

8 Make two handles – one on each side of the bag – or thread a long cord through all four holes and secure the ends with a knot on the inside (or tie in a bow). For each handle cut a length of cord or ribbon long enough to thread through both holes and provide a comfortable handle.

Gift tags
9 Make a gift tag to match or contrast with the gift bag. Laminate a piece of wrapping paper to heavy drawing paper or posterboard, and crease to mark a center fold. Cut around to the shape required, and punch a hole near the fold to hold the tie. Alternatively, cut around the outline of a suitable motif and laminate this to paper or cardboard.

3D découpage

This quick version of an increasingly popular craft uses motifs on wrapping paper to create greeting cards with an added dimension. Specially selected areas are cut out and elevated with tiny sections cut from sticky adhesive pads to make the picture 'come alive'.

Materials
Four or five identical motifs from wrapping paper, posters or notecards
Heavy drawing paper (optional)
Stiff paper or posterboard for base
Spray adhesive
Double sided adhesive pads
Small nail scissors with curved blades

Preparation
1 If you are using thin paper, laminate it to heavy drawing paper. Use the small scissors to cut out one complete design motif. Mount this on the base paper or posterboard with spray adhesive. (Do not cut this to finished size yet.)

Working the design
2 Cover the whole design area with sticky pads, cutting them down to size as necessary. Avoid placing them at the edge of the design where they may show. Cut out another complete motif and position this accurately over the sticky pads.

3 Look at your chosen motif and decide which areas you want to lift forward, bearing in mind that the aim is to lift the subject matter in the foreground closer, so that details which appear closest to you in the picture will be the top layer of your design. Place sticky pads over your selected areas, and cut out the relevant details from the third motif. Stick these over the pads.

4 Continue adding sticky pads to the chosen areas, and cut more details from the fourth motif. Position over the pads. If you

are using a fifth motif, add these details over another layer of sticky pads in the same way.

5 When the design is complete, decide on the finished shape of the greeting card, to show the design off to best advantage. Mark the shape with a pencil and set square, and cut out with a craft knife. Fold to shape.

Cover the whole design area with sticky pads

Place sticky pads over selected areas ready to position the third layer of motifs

Paper lace

Sewing needles are all that is needed to transform a sheet of paper into an intricate piece of lace. Different effects are achieved by pricking along a drawn outline using various sized needles, or by piercing from both sides of the paper. The results can be used to create a picture, or to personalize stationery and wrapping paper with small motifs and borders.

Materials

Heavy drawing paper and another smooth, fairly stiff paper in a toning color
Tracing paper
Padding: thick felt, blanket or folded cloth
Tapestry needle and a darning needle
Large eraser
Nail scissors with curved blades
Set square, ruler, craft knife, clear cellophane tape, spray adhesive

Preparation

1 Make a handle for the needles by embedding each one at opposite ends of the eraser. The larger needle is used to emphasize shapes, and the smaller needle is used for less prominent shapes.

Basic techniques

2 Holes pierced from the wrong side of the paper have greater definition because of their high relief, while holes pierced from the right side are smooth and less obtrusive, so this can be used to give a sense of perspective to the design. Space the holes equally apart, and not too close together, otherwise the paper may tear. Try out effects with the needles on a spare piece of paper.

3 Trace the landscape (see pages 256–7) and the half border pattern on pages 258–9. Re-trace the half border on folded paper to obtain the complete border. Using two different colored pencils, trace the landscape design onto one sheet of tracing paper, and the complete border onto another. These tracings will be the working patterns.

4 Lay the heavy drawing paper on a flat surface, and then lay the tracing of the landscape, with the wrong side facing upwards over this. Attach with clear cellophane tape placed along the top edge. Lay both sheets over the padded surface. Use the tapestry needle to prick out the outline of the large clouds, lamb and the cottage roof. Use the darning needle to prick the outline of the bushes and trees, birds and sun. Carefully remove the tracing paper.

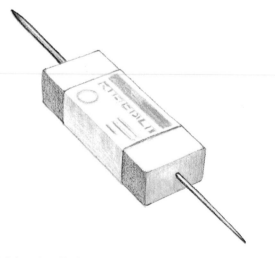

Make a handle for the needles by embedding them into opposite ends of an eraser

Paper lace gift card
Designs for paper lace gift cards can be traced from books, magazines, or from wrapping paper or wallpapers. Mount the pricked paper on a bought blank gift card or make a card by cutting and folding colored heavy drawing paper. It is a good idea to make your card to a standard envelope size.

———— worked from right side   ———— worked from reverse

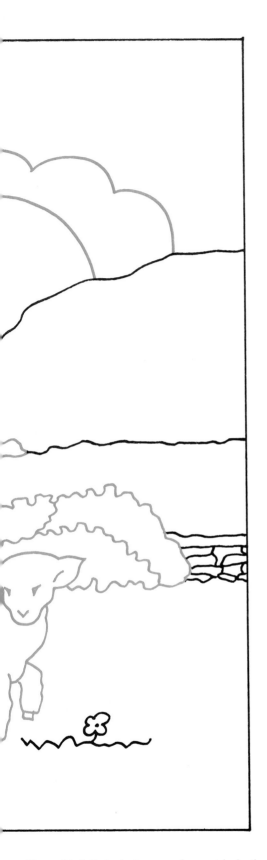

5 Turn the heavy drawing paper over and replace the tracing, carefully lining up the pricked holes. Prick out the rest of the landscape using the large needle to mark the wispy cloudline, the hills, path and top of the wall. Use the smaller needle to mark all the other details. Remove the tracing and set heavy drawing paper aside.

The border

6 Take a colored sheet of paper, and using the border tracing as a guide, mark out the center rectangle. Cut this away with a craft knife. Trim the paper around the rectangle to make a 2in (5cm) border all around. Spray the wrong side of border with adhesive, and position the border over the landscape, using the original tracing as a guide.

7 Place the landscape and border, wrong side facing upwards, to padded surface. Position the border tracing on top, lining up the outline carefully, and prick the design. Use the tapestry needle to mark the large flower outlines, and the straight band nearest the flowers. Use the darning needle to prick the smaller flowers and the leaves. Remove the tracing and turn the work over to the right side.

Trace this full-sized picture and use with the frame on pages 258–9

PAPER LACE BORDER

—————— worked from right side   —————— worked from reverse

center fold

top

8 Re-position the tracing, and use the darning needle to prick out the inner straight band. Mark in the lines on the petals and small scroll shapes. Remove tracing. Carefully cut around the border outline (see broken line) with the curved scissors, cutting to within ¼in (6mm) of the pricked outlines. Frame the picture on a neutral color background to complement the delicate effect.

inner edge

259

Ribbon box

Giftwrap ribbon can be woven and used as a decorative insert for a special giftbox.

Materials
Heavy drawing paper or copy paper
Giftwrap ribbon in six colors
Medium-weight cardboard
Wrapping paper, lining paper
Masking tape
Spray adhesive, clear craft glue

Preparation
1 Decide the area size you are going to weave. Cut the ribbons to a little more than the depth of the area. Tape the ribbons side by side vertically, on heavy drawing paper with the ends level, in a six-color sequence to make the warp.

2 Keeping to the same color sequence, weave the same number of ribbons in and out across the warp (these horizontal ribbons are called the weft). Tape the ends.

3 Use masking tape to mask off the design areas, and cut out the woven square cutting through the center of the securing tapes. Trim away paper underneath, so that weave is supported on the edges only by the tape. Place the work wrong side up and spray the back with adhesive. Press, sticky side down, onto another piece of heavy drawing paper and trim around.

Making the box
4 For this design, start by making the box lid, as this is custom-made to fit the woven insert. The lid is made from one piece of cardboard. On cardboard, draw the central square shape for the woven insert. To do this, measure and mark the size of the woven square within the masked area. Decide on size of surrounding lid, and mark this onto cardboard. Extend edges to make box sides and add a flap at each end of two side pieces. Cut out the central

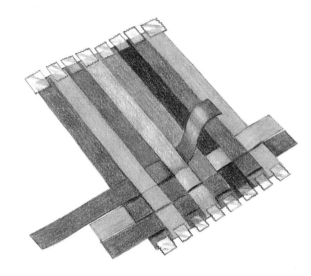

Tape the warp ribbons to paper, weave the weft ribbons in and out

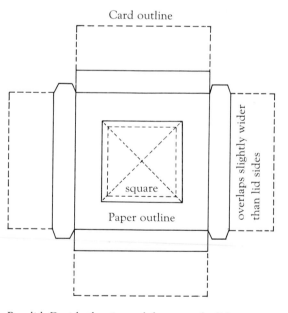

Box lid: Decide the size and draw out the lid square, extend the edges for the box sides, add a flap at the ends of the side pieces

square and discard. Cut around the lid outline and gently score the fold lines around the lid top and for flaps.

5 Open the lid flat, and spray the scored side with adhesive. Press flat onto the wrong side of wrapping paper. Cut out around the edge allowing an overlap on each side to reach around to inside the lid. Cut across the center square diagonally, and turn back the paper. Trim and glue to the wrong side, and glue the side overlaps to the wrong side with clear glue. Spread glue on the side overlaps and press to the inside edges, then stick the paper overlaps in place as side linings.

6 Run a line of glue around the masking tape on the woven insert, and stick in place on the wrong side of the lid. Line the lid.

7 Make the box base. Measure the inside box lid, and draw a square a little smaller than the lid measurement onto cardboard. This is the base. Extend the lines to the required depth, as for the lid, to make the box sides. Add flaps and score. Glue the box to paper and cover in the same way, allowing extra paper at the sides for overlaps and full linings.

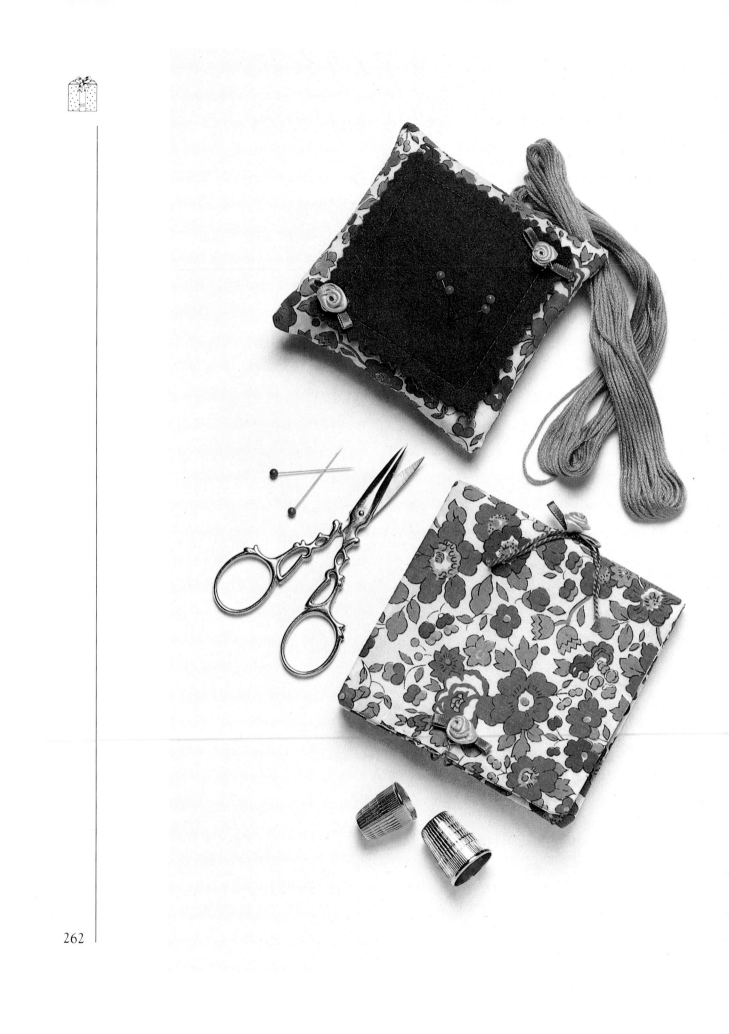

Better techniques

Most of the equipment that you need to make the items in this book you will have in the home, while the remainder are readily available from fabric or craft shops.

NO-SEW CRAFTS
Tools and equipment
Most equipment required for no-sew crafts is readily available, and you will have most of it already. There are a few specialist tools, however, which provide for greater creative possibilities, and help to give papercraft items a more professional finish.

The work surface is important. This should be at a good working height, flat and stable. You will need a protective surface to use over the work top, to protect it from cuts and scratches when using craft knives. A sheet of thick cardboard is a suitable protection but should be replaced frequently as the surface will become pitted from successive knife cuts. It is worth investing in a special cutting mat. This has a surface which 'heals itself' after every cut, and thus remains smooth, and will not distort subsequent cuts made over it.

Cutting tools
You will need two kinds of craft knives: a heavy duty knife, like an X-acto knife, for cutting thick cardboard, and a small knife, preferably a scalpel, for posterboard and paper. Use straight blades, as these suit most tasks, and replace them often for the best results. Needless to say, these knives require care when in use. You should always cut straight lines by lining up the knife against a firm straight edge. Use a metal ruler for this rather than a plastic or wood ruler, as these materials can easily catch in the blade.

You will need several pairs of sharp scissors. Have a pair of fairly small, easy-to-handle scissors with straight pointed blades for most cutting jobs, a longer broad-bladed pair for general cutting and stretching paper, and nail scissors with curved blades for cutting around intricate shapes. A pair of tweezers is useful for handling small cutout shapes. Other useful cutting tools are hole punchers.

Other equipment
Precise paper folding and creasing is important. One really useful specialty tool for marking fold lines on paper is a bookbinder's bone folder, which looks rather like a small modeling tool. This is drawn along against a straight edge and leaves a gentle groove ready for folding. You can improvise, however, by using a knitting needle or a blunt, curve-bladed table knife, a letter opener or any other tool which creases rather than pierces the paper surface.

Drawing aids required include a compass, a set square and a ruler with small measurement markings, plus paper clips, and a stapler. You also need a pencil sharpener and a selection of hard and soft pencils, colored pencils and felt tipped markers. A good quality eraser is essential.

Using spray adhesive

This very useful adhesive is ideal in projects which use wrapping papers. An important advantage over other glues is its delayed sticking time, which means that sprayed papers can be re-positioned if necessary. Use spray adhesive to make thin papers more durable by laminating them to a thicker paper like heavy drawing paper. When laminating very small paper shapes, the spraying can be done with the paper resting on an expanse of newspapers. However it is best to make a spray booth from a cardboard box, as this will protect surrounding surfaces and furnishings. Choose a box large enough to comfortably hold the work for spraying.

Place a large box on its side and surround it with old newspapers. Place the cardboard or paper shape as far inside as possible. To spray, hold the can upright and spray evenly over the surface with a sweeping motion. Handle the sticky work as little as possible when transferring it to the work surface. Lay the work sticky side up, and press the corresponding paper piece over. Smooth to stick, then trim around the shape as necessary. Turn over and smooth the surface flat.

Carbon paper is useful for transferring designs, but as the traced outlines cannot be removed, only use well-used carbon paper for tracings where the remaining outline does not matter.

Mark fold lines with a bookbinder's bone folder

Paints

Paints used for crafts include poster paints, acrylics, water colors and designer gouache. You can also use household latex paints and model maker's enamel paints, as well as multipurpose metallic paint. Varnish for finishing and protecting work can be gloss, semi gloss or flat finish. Use a varnish suitable for paper, or a household varnish applied to the previously protected surface (see below). Paint brushes should include a range of watercolor brushes, and small household paint brushes.

To keep the nozzle of spray adhesive from clogging up after use, hold the can nozzle down and spray until the spray stops, then wipe over to clean the outside. If the spray has already clogged, wipe over with a cotton swab dipped in nail polish remover, then if necessary, repierce the hole with a needle point.

Make a spraying booth from a cardboard box

A spray fixative can be used to protect finished work. This leaves a protective sheen on paper, making it less likely to mark or stain. Fixative can also be used on lightweight papers and paper printed on both sides – like magazine pages – to protect them from becoming transparent through over-wetting with glue or varnish.

Tapes and adhesives

Choose the right adhesive tape for the job. You may require transparent clear cellophane tape, double-sided clear cellophane tape, masking tape, or gummed brown paper tape. Specialist tapes like stretchy flowermaking tape (gutta tape) are available for binding wires and stems.

White glue is a multi-purpose, easy-to-use adhesive, which can be used both as a glue and a varnish. Although white, the glue dries transparent and gives a glossy protective surface. It can be used full strength or diluted with water. Clear, quick-drying and non-trailing craft glue is a good multi-purpose adhesive for cardboard and paper. Use a glue spreader for an even coverage. A glue stick is required for some paper projects. This type of adhesive comes in a roll-up tube and is easy to control. An advantage is that unlike most other adhesives, it does not dampen the paper. Superglues are used to bond different types of material together. Use these for joining metal to paper for instance, as when attaching jewelry components. One of the most useful adhesives, and probably the most widely used throughout the book, is spray adhesive. This allows you to laminate large or very small areas of paper together without stretching or dampening the paper. Spray adhesive should be used in a confined space to prevent the sticky mist settling on surrounding surfaces.

Checklist
Cutting out scissors
Small pointed scissors
Nail scissors
Paper scissors
Craft knife
Scalpel holder and blade
Coping saw
Tape measure
Yard stick
Metal edged rule and cutting board
Fabric marking pen
Tailor's chalk
Squared paper
Soft and hard pencils
Tracing paper
Latex adhesive
Spray fixative
All-purpose glue
White glue
Dressmakers' carbon paper, dark and
   light colors
Glass-headed pins
Assortment of needles for sewing,
   embroidery
Pins
Soft cotton
All-purpose sewing threads
Small thumbtacks
Posterboard for templates
Polyester toy filling
Watercolor paints
Poster colors
Modeler's enamels
Brushes and brush cleaner

Cutting paper and cardboard

To cut thick cardboard, lay it flat on a protective surface. Draw the pattern outline directly onto the cardboard. Use a set square and ruler to check right angles and parallel lines. Line up the straight metal edge against the line to be cut. Press the craft knife against the metal edge, and firmly draw the knife towards you, keeping an even pressure on the straight edge to keep it still. Score the cutting line gently to mark it (and if only marking fold lines) then still with the straight edge in position, cut along the line again, pressing harder to cut through the cardboard. To cut around curves, mark the shape lightly with the knife point, and cut around making sure that the free hand is pressing firmly on the cardboard to keep it still, and that fingers are not in line with the knife, should it slip.

To use a scalpel on paper, follow the same basic process. When cutting small shapes with right angles and tight curves, start by piercing the corner point of each shape with the point of the blade, and cut away from the corner, drawing the knife towards you. This should ensure neatly cut points.

When cutting small shapes with a scalpel, start by piercing the corner point, then cut toward you

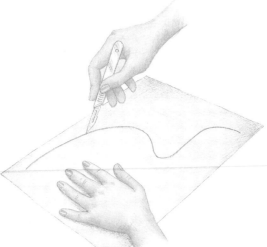

To cut around curves, mark the shape lightly with the knife point

When using scissors to cut paper shapes it is sometimes desirable to soften the cut edge, particularly with thick paper and when cutting shapes for découpage, where the paper edge should be as thin and unobtrusive as possible. To do this, hold the paper right side facing you and roughly cut around the required shape, leaving a generous border around the main subject matter. Now hold the scissor blades at a slight angle away from you, and cut around again at the required edge. By cutting the paper at an angle you create a bevelled edge, making the harsh cutting line less noticeable. Use curved nail scissors, the blades positioned appropriately, to cut out very small shapes.

Covering corners

Whether covering folder sides or boxes you can achieve neat, professional looking corners by following one of these methods. The first, folded method is more suitable for thin papers. The second, cut and dart method can be used for thicker papers, as bulk is reduced, and it gives neat covered corners on the edges of thick cardboard, where it is sometimes difficult to avoid the cardboard from showing through. However, if this does ever happen you can insert a little patch of matching paper over the corner, underneath the covering paper. Both of these methods use either a glue stick or a clear quick-drying craft glue to secure the corners and overlaps.

Folded corners

Working on the reverse of the cardboard, crease the overlap diagonally at the corner as shown, and glue the overlap onto the cardboard. Crease the folded paper gently at the cardboard edge and fold each overlap onto the cardboard. Glue in place.

Cut and dart corners
Working on the reverse of the cardboard, make a cut in line with each straight edge as shown then cut a narrow strip within that, tapering towards the corner of the cardboard. Cut the overlaps (shaded areas on the diagram) away at each side. Gently apply glue to the center strip, and smooth it onto the card. Press the strip flat to mold to the corner shape. Spread glue on the shaped overlaps, and press onto the card.

Stretching and curling paper
Paper grain can be used to advantage for molding paper to a required shape. One of the easiest ways to shape paper is to gently stretch and curl it over a scissor blade. Papers that respond well to this are art and tissue papers, heavy drawing and most lightweight papers, as well as crepe paper and paper ribbon. To stretch the paper, cut out the shape with the grain running in the direction to be stretched. Hold the paper in one hand and the open scissor blade in the other. Gently pull the blade across the underside of the paper, from the base to the tip of the shape. Repeat until the paper is curled sufficiently.

To stretch crepe paper across its grain, to mold it into a rounded curve as for making

Folded corner: Crease the overlap diagonally on the corner (left) then crease and fold the overlap on to the card (right)

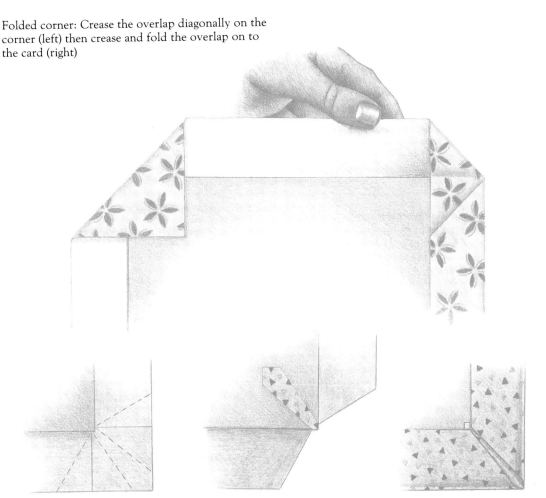

Cut and dart corner: Cut the overlaps away at each side (left).
Glue the center strips on to the cardboard (middle) then glue overlaps

Gently pull the blade across the underside of the paper until the paper curls

After cupping a flower petal, shape the edges by curling them over a scissor blade

flower petals, cut out the required shape with the grain running opposite to the required stretch direction. Hold each side of the shape between thumb and fingers, and gently stretch, stroking the paper sideways with the thumbs to mold it. The upper and lower edges of the shape can be further shaped by curling over a scissor blade if required.

Pleating paper
Accordion pleats are equal size pleats, and are used in three projects in this book. The pleats are easy to make, relying on careful measuring and accurate folding. Cut a strip of paper to the required depth. Use a set square to check the right angle at one end of the strip and a ruler and pencil to measure and mark out equally spaced divisions along the top and lower edge.

Join these marks up with a ruler and pencil, then gently score along each line. Fold up the pleats. To join pleats, simply overlap the ends by an entire pleat, arranging the join so that the edge on the right side is hidden in the valley of the fold. Secure behind with glue.

Join the pleat marks with pencil and ruler, then score each line

Papier mâché

Papier mâché, which literally means 'chewed paper', can be worked in various ways. The projects in this book are all made using small strips of glue-soaked paper. Strips are overlapped and arranged over a mold (which can be anything from a bowl to a banana), until the layers are thick enough to hold the shape. This is usually possible after six or eight layers have been added. The work is left to dry completely, and is then removed from the mold, ready to be decorated. Old newspapers are a traditional favorite for providing the strips, as these are readily available, cost nothing, and are easy to handle. Decorative papers can be added as a final decoration, or if preferred, to make the entire object. The instructions here are for working the basic papier mâché strip technique over a mold. In projects follow individual project instructions for special details relating to those particular designs.

Basic technique

If using molds to make an open object like a dish or bowl, the mold should be a shape which allows for easy removal of the finished papier mâché. Avoid molds which have a lip or rim at the top edge. Glass mixing bowls and overproof dishes often make suitable molds. Other mold objects, like fresh fruit, require a different approach. When using entire shapes like these, the papier mâché has to be cut away after it is dry. To do this the finished shape is cut through all around with a craft knife. The two halves are removed from the mold, and the two papier mâché shapes are joined together again with glued paper strips placed across the cut edges.

Some pieces of work like the papier mâché bracelets and brooches (on page 218) and the picture frame (on page 186) are molded over cardboard shapes. These are left in place to form a rigid base for the design.

Preparing molds: It is necessary to lubricate the mold before applying the paper strips so that the finished papier mâché can be removed easily. Smear the mold surface liberally with petroleum jelly. If it is necessary to remove the papier mâché at any time during the drying process, re-grease the mold before replacing the work.

Working with a mold: Protect the work surface with old newspapers. When using a dish or bowl-shape molds, invert the mold over a suitable prop like a can or mug – any object tall enough to raise the mold off the work surface and keep it stable.

Preparing paper strips: Tear paper into small strips about ½in (12mm) wide × 2in (5cm) long. This size strip will mold well around most curves. (For larger or smaller projects adapt the strip size.) As a guide, the strips should adhere to the mold without pleating or distorting.

Preparing adhesive: Wallpaper paste (without fungicide) mixed to full strength is popular for working papier mâché. Drying time is slightly longer, however, with a very wet adhesive like this. Undiluted white glue can be added to the paste to stiffen it slightly, and to speed drying time, or you can use white glue on its own, diluted with water to a stiff cream consistency. A white glue solution produces papier mâché with a light, almost plastic feel to it.

Trim the uneven edge of a papier mâché bowl with scissors

Applying the strips: Starting at the top of the greased mold (the base), first use water only to dampen the strips, and smooth each one in place, overlapping edges slightly, to build a layer reaching downwards to the outside edge. Allow the strips to overlap the edge slightly, as this can be trimmed later. Apply a second layer of strips, this time using adhesive, and work the strips around the bowl in the other direction. This helps to build a firm, strong web. Paint glue over the surface, and smooth with your hands to remove any air bubbles. Do this after applying each layer of strips. Add another layer of glued strips, working downwards in the same direction as the first layer. Continue in this way until six or eight layers are in place. (If the bowl seems fragile when dry, you can always add more strips.) Finish with a coat of glue.

Drying papier mâché: Papier mâché can take several days to dry so be patient if you want successful results. Keep the mold on the prop, and leave the work to dry naturally in a warm, airy place. To hasten the process, you can place papier mâché on fireproof props in an oven, set at lowest heat. Place objects modeled all over a mold on a mesh surface such as a wire rack.

Removing work from mold: To unmold a bowl shape, gently insert a thin knife, such as a palette knife, between the bowl and the mold and slide around to break any vacuum which may have formed. Gently ease the papier mâché away, and place on work surface. Trim the uneven edge with scissors, or leave in its natural state if preferred. Check for any thin patches, and build these up with extra strips. Leave to dry. Smooth any uneven patches with sandpaper. To unmold solid shapes (such as fruit) cut around and join with glued paper strips (see page 210).

Decorating papier mâché: Paint with a coat of white latex paint, or another light, opaque undercoat such as poster or acrylic paint. You can draw designs and paint on to this, or add collage decoration. Work on the inside of a bowl shape, then invert it on to a prop, and decorate the outside. If you are using paints, make sure each color is dry before proceeding to the next. Paint awkward shapes bit by bit, first painting one side and then the other, to avoid fingerprint marks. Finish by painting with one or two thin coats of varnish, applying it stage by stage. Most pieces can be left to dry on a wire rack.

REMOVING GLUES

Glue manufacturers will always help with advice about solvents for their products and some will supply these solvents direct if you write to them. In general, the first step in glue first aid is to scape off any deposit and then proceed as follows:

Clear glue:
On skin, wash first, then remove any residue with nail polish remover. On clothing or furnishings, hold a pad or absorbent rag on the underside, dab with non-oily nail polish remover on the right side.

Epoxy glue:
Lighter fuel or cellulose thinners will remove glue from the hands. On fabrics, hold a rag pad under the glue stain, dab with cellulose thinners on the right side. On synthetic fibers, use lighter fuel.

Adhesive tape residue:
White spirit or cellulose thinners may do it. Or try nail varnish remover. Adhesives vary and you will have to experiment.

Latex glue:
Lift off as much as possible before the glue hardens. Keep the glue soft with cold water and rub with a cloth. Treat any stains with liquid dry cleaner. Scrape off any deposits with a pencil eraser.

To paint or varnish beads: Select a skewer or knitting needle to fit tightly through the bead, so that the bead cannot slip around. Lubricate the skewer with petroleum jelly and thread the beads onto this, leaving a gap between each one. Hold the skewer in one hand, and paint with the other. Dry by balancing the skewer between two objects, or push the end securely into piece of modeling clay. Leave to dry.

Making cardboard boxes

The boxes in this book are made in two basic ways. Boxes made from posterboard are mostly made from a single sheet of posterboard which is accurately scored along marked lines and folded into shape. Integral tabs, which are angled or curved to

To paint paper beads, thread them on a skewer and balance across cans

fit into the box without distorting it, are glued and pressed to the box sides to hold its shape. Larger boxes – too big to cut from a single sheet of posterboard – and those made from thick cardboard, are usually made by joining each side piece separately. Each section is glued to the other, and the sides are reinforced with gummed tape.

With all adhesives, read the manufacturer's instructions carefully before use, and have the necessary solvents at hand to cope with accidental spills.

With most designs it is a good idea to make the box lid after the main box is covered. This is to ensure a good fit, taking into consideration the thickness of the cardboard and the covering paper.

To make a lid, (which can often be cut from a single piece of cardboard) take the outside measurement of each box side and mark this accurately with a set square and ruler onto the center of a piece of cardboard. Measure a tiny amount extra all around this shape (about $\frac{1}{8}$in (3mm) is usually enough) to allow for the thickness of the covering paper. This shape is the lid top. Extend the lines to make side pieces from this basic shape, adding tabs to each side of two sides if you are using posterboard. Cut out and construct in the same way as for the box. Check the fit before gluing the lid sides, by holding them in place with a little clear cellophane tape. For lids made piece-by-piece, measure for the lid top in the same way.

Covering boxes

Boxes can be covered with paper by adding pieces separately to each side. This is necessary for large boxes, where a single sheet may not reach all the way around. When covering a box in this way, the paper sides are cut with an overlap turning at top and base, and an overlap on each end of two sides. The other two sides are added last and are cut with side edges flush with the box sides. Corners of overlaps are trimmed diagonally to fit over edges neatly, then a base piece is fitted. Box linings are added in much the same way – just omit the top overlap. Alternatively, the box sides can be covered with one long strip and a side overlap. The finished edge is placed onto the overlap, flush with the box. The turnings for the top and base are the same, and these are snipped at each corner when fitting to the wrong side.

Gift wrapping

Papercrafts lend themselves naturally to gift wrapping – box making and covering boxes, pleating paper, paper freizes and patchwork, paper flowers and lace, and paper weaving. Once you have familiarized yourself with the different techniques, you can adapt your skills to creative gift wrapping.

Wrapping plain boxes is an art in itself and lovely effects can be achieved quite simply through the careful choice of paper and ribbon.

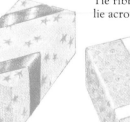

Fold the edge of the overlap under

Fold the top flap down the bottom flap up

Boxes
Square or rectangular box

Make sure that you have enough wrapping paper. If necessary, tape sheets together. Use a glue stick (or double-sided tape) for sealing edges. Transparent cellophane tape always shows and can look messy.

Lay the box on the wrong side of the paper. Bring up the sides and then trim the

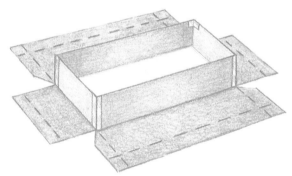

To cover a box, place it on the paper and draw extending lines outwards. Cut to an angle at the corners.

Glue the overlaps to the inside and ends of the box

Tie ribbons to lie across the corners

Arrange the ribbon so it crosses off center

overlap to about 2in (5cm). Fold the edge of the overlap under. The paper should extend over the ends a little more than half the depth of the box. Glue or tape the overlap down. Fold in the sides first, then the top flap down and the bottom flap up. Glue, or fasten with a piece of double sided tape placed under the flaps so that it does not show.

Round boxes
Trace the bottom and top of the box on the wrong side of the paper. Cut out 2 circles. Measure the depth of the box and the circumference. Cut a piece of wrapping paper to the box depth measurement plus 1in (2.5cm) with 1in (2.5cm) extra on the length for overlap. Place the paper around the box, fold under the edge of the overlap and glue. Snip into the extra paper at the top and bottom edges of the box to make tabs. Fold them in. Spread glue around the edges of the two paper circles and press them onto the tabs.

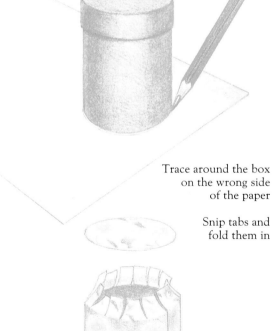

Trace around the box
on the wrong side
of the paper

Snip tabs and
fold them in

Original wraps
Although well-chosen wrapping paper and ribbons will usually produce attractive effects, for really original packages you should treat every giftwrap as an artist treats a canvas. Look through this book and think about the things you can use as decoration, other than ribbons and bows. You could pleat heavy drawing paper and patterned wrapping paper into miniature fans and tie them on with ribbons. Or cut shapes from white paper and prick them into paper lace with festive designs. You might make a string of paper beads with red, green and gold paper and loop them across the package. Paper flowers used singly or in posies look pretty on both summer and wintertime gifts.

Tie on miniature
paper-fans

Loop paper beads
across the parcel

Decorate gifts with
paper flowers

Wrapping plants

Plants in pots are welcome and popular gifts and are not difficult to package attractively. You need a large sheet of stiff posterboard, colored on one side or with wrapping paper laminated to it. Stand the pot in the middle of the posterboard on the wrong side. Hold a ruler against the pot on four sides and mark the posterboard. Join the marks and pencil the square. Remove the pot and score along the lines of the

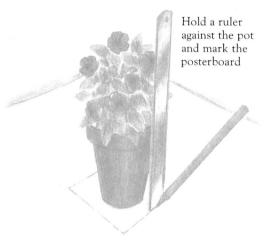

Hold a ruler against the pot and mark the posterboard

square. Next, measure the height of the pot and the plant together. Mark this measurement out from the sides of the square. Draw lines from the corners of the square to the marks. Cut out. Punch a single hole in each point about ⅔in (18mm) from the tip. Stand the pot on the penciled square, fold up the four sides and tie the box together through the punched holes with ribbon. Tie more ribbons with streamer ends to cascade down the sides of the box.

Draw lines from the corners to the center marks

Ribbons and bows

Gift ribbon that sticks to itself when moistened is used to make decorative rosettes and bows. Use single colors or mix two or three shades together.

Rosette

This bow can be made with woven gift ribbon also. Loop the ribbon as shown, tie in the middle with another piece of ribbon. Spread out the loops. Fish-tail the ribbon ends.

This design can also be turned into a star by cutting each of the loops and fish-tailing the ends.

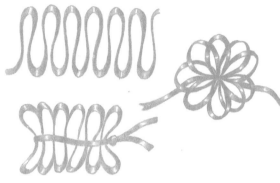

Petals

Moisten the end of a length of gift ribbon and form a small ring. Wind the ribbon around, moisten the surface and make another, slightly larger ring. Continue making rings until you have formed a petal shape. Pinch the tips. Petals can be used flat, secured to the package with double sided tape, to make a flower shape. Or several can be fastened together, points upwards, with long ribbon ends.

Tie ribbons through the punched holes

Flat bow

Use either gift ribbon or woven ribbon for this bow.

Cut a strip of ribbon and join both ends in the middle. Cut a short piece and bind it over the middle, joining the ends on the underside of the bow.

Make a bigger bow by cutting a long strip of ribbon and gluing down a loop at one end. Fold the ribbon to make another loop, facing the other way, glue at the center. Continue making loops to either side of the middle, each slightly shorter than the ones before. Three or four loops is sufficient. Cut a short strip and bind the middle.

Daisy

Cut 4 pieces of gift ribbon about 8in (20cm) long. Lay the pieces in a star shape. Moisten and join at the center. Bring the ends up and fasten together. Moisten the inside of the ball shape and push the top and bottom together firmly until they stick.

Flat bow

Chrysanthemum

Cut ½in (12mm)-wide gift ribbon into 16in (40cm) lengths. Cut the strips down the middle. Moisten the ends of strips and join them. Turn the ring into a figure-eight, moisten to hold the shape. Join 2 figure-eights with glue. Make more figure-eights and add them, laying them first one way, then the other until a chrysanthemum has been formed. You will need about 14 to get the effect.

Daisy

Rosette

Petals

Chrysanthemum

NEEDLECRAFTS
Materials and equipment
Cutting tools

Scissors: For basic sewing you need two pairs of scissors. A large pair for cutting out and a small sharply-pointed pair for snipping threads, etc. Scissors must be sharp especially when cutting out fabrics. A good pair will give you clean, cutting lines rather than tearing the fabric.

Keep your scissors sharp. Most types can be sharpened on a kitchen knife sharpener. Never use dressmaking scissors for cutting out heavy paper or cardboard because the cutting edge will be damaged, making the scissors useless for cutting fabrics subsequently. Avoid cutting across pins when cutting out as this can damage the blades.

For cutting out paper and cardboard use a good pair of household scissors. For purely decorative purposes it is a good idea to have a pair of pinking shears, but do not use them for cutting out as they will not give an accurate outline. Pinking shears are also useful for trimming seam allowances to minimize fraying.

Measuring equipment

It is essential to have a good tape measure in your work box. This must be made from non-stretch material and have metal ends.

When cutting out large pieces of fabric you might find a yard stick useful.

Marking aids

From time to time you will need to mark the fabric with patterns and designs ready for cutting out. The easiest way to mark outlines on fabric is with a fabric marking pen or with tailors' chalk. Both pens and chalk come in a variety of colors, so choose one a shade darker than the fabric. The chalk will easily brush off the fabric and the pen marks can be removed by washing or, with some types, will disappear after 48 hours.

When you have to mark an appliqué or embroidery design onto fabric, use a sheet of dressmakers' carbon paper.

Sewing equipment

Pins: There is a good variety of pins on the market for different types of sewing. For most sewing, use a fine, standard length pin (but check to make sure that they are sharp). Blunt pins can snag the fabric, so discard these if you find them in the box. When working with some of the heavier craft materials use a thicker household pin, and if you are always dropping pins on the floor, buy glass-headed pins because these are easier to see against the carpet.

Needles: Needles are divided into groups, depending on their use. For general sewing use 'sharps', available in sizes 3–10 (the higher the number the finer the needle). If you prefer a shorter needle, use a 'between'.

When doing hand sewing, wear a thimble on the middle finger of the sewing hand. This will help push the needle through tough fabrics.

If you have a problem threading needles use a needle threader.

Sewing threads

One of the most important materials in a sewing project is the thread. Always match the type of thread to the fabric, such as silk with silk and cotton with cotton. For mixed-fiber fabrics choose an all-purpose thread. It is important that you match thread to the color of the fabric. The various brands available all have good ranges of colors from which to choose and, as a general rule, you should go for one in a shade darker than the fabric. If you like to baste seams before stitching them, use a soft, loosely-twisted basting thread.

Fabrics

Before you start any project, look through your remnants. You will probably find one that you can use. When you are buying fabric for a dress or making a homesewing project, it is a good idea to buy an extra half yard. This, together with any remnants can often be put to good use, such as a set of matching accessories for a dressing table or some colorful items for the kitchen.

When selecting fabrics, remember that closely woven fabrics tend to fray less than loosely woven types. These fabrics are also easier to sew and generally give a good result. Make sure they have easy-care properties, so that they can be washed without the colors running and need little ironing.

Colors will be a personal choice, but when looking at a printed fabric, bear in mind the finished size of the project and avoid using large prints on small items. Most of the projects in this book will look best if they are made up in small sprig fabrics. The scale of checked and striped fabrics must be also noted; go for the small check ginghams rather than the larger versions whenever possible.

Interfacing

When a fabric requires extra body, use a layer of interfacing behind the fabric. Interfacing can be simply a layer of a thinner fabric, basted to the top fabric but fusible interfacings are easier to work with. Non-woven fusible interfacings can be bought in various weights.

Batting

Batting is the layer of fabric that is sandwiched between two other fabrics in quilting. Washable, polyester batting comes in a range of different weights from light to an extra heavyweight (only used in upholstery). Use a lightweight batting to give fabric extra body, and the medium and heavyweight versions for quilting, or when an extra layer for warmth is required.

To make diamond quilting even easier, there is an interfacing which is ready-marked with quilting lines. This is fused to the wrong side of fabric and then machine-quilting is worked over the marked lines.

Decorative trimmings

Small projects often look prettier with the addition of a decorative trim. Ribbons and braids come in most widths and the color ranges are extensive so it is usually easy to find a good match. Besides plain ribbons in polyester satin, grosgrain, velvet and taffeta, there are printed ribbons, jacquard weaves and a variety of decoratively-edged ribbons to be found. Attach narrow ribbons and braids by stitching them down the center. With wider ribbons, machine-stitch down both edges, always stitching in the same direction to prevent puckering.

Ready-made bias strips are useful for finishing raw edges decoratively. These come in cotton or satin in plain colors and are also available in a pretty range of cotton prints.

Lace too comes in a variety of patterns and widths. Choose cotton laces if the item is to be ironed. Pretty cotton eyelet is available flat or pre-gathered, some for insertion and for beading with ribbon. Some colored laces are in the shops but if you need a touch of color cotton lace dyes very easily.

Beads and sequins are lovely to work with and again the ranges of colors, sizes and types are extensive.

Fancy buttons can also be used as decorative trim, especially when they have a shank rather than central holes. Modern button ranges come in hundreds of different shapes – flowers, tiny animals and insects, ships, airplanes and steam trains, fun foods, initials, suns, moons and stars.

Other useful trims are ribbon flowers, which can be bought in mixed packets of different sizes.

PATTERN MAKING

Patterns are generally given in two forms, direct tracings and graph patterns.

Direct tracing patterns

To use these, you will need sheets of tracing paper. Lay the tracing paper over the book page and tape it down at the edges. Trace the image with a sharply pointed pencil.

Very simple shapes, such as squares or circles, may be drawn directly onto the wrong side of smooth fabrics, using either a soft pencil or dressmakers' chalk pencil. If fabrics are very thin and transparent, full-size patterns can be direct-traced from the page, using a finely sharpened hard pencil or a colored embroidery pencil. Another useful marking device is a pen which has air-soluble ink in it. After tracing a pattern the line remains on the fabric for a short time and, usually after sewing, it has disappeared.

Preparing patterns

Trace full-sized patterns on tracing paper, spacing pieces about an inch (2.5cm) apart. When a pattern piece is larger, it may be split on the page and arrows or dotted lines will indicate where the pieces are to be joined. Trace the largest piece, move the tracing paper and trace the remaining section.

Some pattern pieces may be shown as one half only. To make a complete pattern, lay the folded edge of your tracing paper against the fold line on the master pattern (this will usually be marked 'place to fold'). Trace the outline, unfold the paper, refold and trace again.

Graph patterns

These patterns are given reduced in size on a squared grid. A scale is given and, to produce a full-sized pattern, you need squared dressmakers' paper marked with squares of the same scale. This paper is sold in large sheets, several to a packet, and can be obtained from a fabric store.

To reproduce a graph pattern you copy the lines on your pattern paper, square for square.

Transferring patterns

Patterns are transferred to the fabric with dressmakers' carbon paper. This is sold in sheets in packets of three or four colors, red, blue, yellow and white. A sheet is slipped between the pattern and fabric, and then the lines traced over with a tracing tool or a hard pencil.

Reading patterns

Before using a pattern it is important that you study the information given on it. This may take the form of words, numerals, letters, arrows and other symbols and is provided so that you cut out the correct number of pieces, arrange the fabric with the grain in the right direction and cut along folded fabric or from doubled fabric when required.

EMBROIDERY STITCHES

There are literally hundreds of embroidery stitches to choose from when you are decorating fabric.

Satin stitch

This is used for filling shapes. Work stitches evenly and so that they touch. Bring the needle through at A, insert it at B and bring it through again at C.

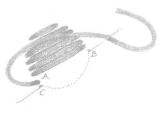

Straight stitch

Straight stitches can be used to fill shapes or singly. Stitches can also be worked in an eight-point star. Bring the needle through at A, insert it at B and bring it through again at C.

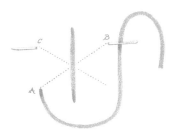

Back stitch

This stitch, properly worked, looks like machine-stitching and can be used for seaming. Bring the needle through at A, insert it at B and bring it out at C in front of A.

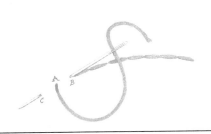

Stem stitch

This is often recommended for working flower stems and for outlining. Bring the needle through at A, the thread below the needle. Insert it at B and bring it through again at C.

Chain stitch

Bring the needle through at A and, with the thread below the needle, insert it beside A at B. The thread forms a loop. Bring the needle through at C, pull through gently, ready to start the next chain stitch.

Detached chain stitch

To work this stitch, from C, work a tying stitch over the loop.

French knot

French knots are a decorative stitch. Bring the needle through at A, wind the thread around the needle twice and then insert the point at B, close by A. Pull the thread through so that the knot tightens on the fabric surface.

SEWING STITCHES

Basting: This is a temporary stitch used to hold two layers of fabric together while the permanent stitching is worked.

Fasten the thread end either with a knot or with a double backstitch on the spot. Then take ½in (12mm)-long stitches through the fabrics. Once the main stitching is complete, snip off the end knot (or unpick the backstitches) and pull out the basting threads.

Running stitch: This stitch is used for gathering or when stitching fine seams by hand. Work from the right to the left. Begin with 2 or 3 backstitches on the spot. Pass the needle in and out of the fabric, making small, evenly-spaced stitches about ⅛in (3mm) long. When gathering, make sure that the thread is long enough to complete the area to be gathered.

Running stitch and gathering

Backstitch: This stitch looks like machine stitching when properly worked and is very strong and hard wearing. It is an ideal stitch to use when sewing seams by hand. Work from right to left. Begin with 2 or 3 stitches on the spot then work a running stitch and a space, take the needle back over the space, bringing it out the same distance away.

Slipstitch: This is a neat, almost invisible stitch that is used to catch a folded edge in place, such as when applying bias strip, or when joining seam edges from the right side. Work from right to left. Fasten the thread with a knot held inside the fold of the fabric. Bring the needle through and pick up a tiny stitch below the folded edge, then run the needle through the folded

edge. Bring the needle through and continue in the same way.

Working slipstitch

Herringbone stitch: This is a strong stitch used to catch 2 pieces of batting together or to hold non-fusible interfacing in place. Work from left to right, always with the needle point to the left. Secure the thread just below the hem with 2 or 3 backstitches on the spot, bring the needle through and take the needle up diagonally across the hem and work a straight stitch from right to left, the thread over the needle. Take the needle down diagonally to the right, below the hem, and make another straight stitch. Take the needle up diagonally across the hem, and make a straight stitch.

SEAMS

Seam allowances

Always read through pattern instructions to check whether the pattern includes a seam allowance or if one is to be added when cutting out.

Rouleaux

Lengths of bias-cut fabric are made into tubing and then sewn into loops for fastening edges. Cut 1in (2.5cm)-wide bias strips into lengths plus ¼in (6mm) turnings at both ends. Baste the raw edges together with ¼in (6mm) seams, stitch the seam and then turn the tube right side out. Press only along the seam edge.

Pinning and basting

Many dressmakers pin pieces of fabric together and then start machine-stitching without basting. If you feel confident about doing this, by all means work in this way. Basting is helpful when complicated pieces are to be joined and helps you to stitch a straight seam. To baste, thread a needle with soft basting thread and knot the end. Work medium length running stitches just inside the stitching line, removing pins as you go. Finish with a backstitch, trim off the knot and pull out the basting thread.

Plain flat seam: Place the two pieces of fabric with right sides together. Pin and baste ⅝in (15mm) from the edge. Machine-stitch following the basting line working a few stitches in reverse at each end of the seam to secure the thread ends. Press the seam open. Neaten the raw edges to prevent fraying with zigzag stitch. Alternatively the edges can be cut with pinking shears or can be bound with bias binding.

Right-angled corner: Stitch up to the corner then, with the needle still in the fabric, raise the foot and turn the fabric 90°. Lower the foot and continue stitching.

Sharp-angled corner: Work 1 or 2 stitches across the corner, before continuing along stitching the next side. Trim the seam allowance back around the point.

Curves: After stitching, snip into outward curves and cut small notches from inward curves. This enables the fabric to lie flat.

French seam: This self-neatening seam is very hardwearing. Place the 2 fabric pieces with wrong sides facing. Pin, baste and stitch the seam ¼in (6mm) from the edge. Trim the seam allowance back to ⅛in (3mm). Press the seam open. Fold right sides together, with the stitching right on the fold. Press. Stitch again ⅜in (9mm) from the folded edge.

Wrong sides facing, stitch ¼in (6mm) from edge

Trim the seam allowance to ⅛in (3mm)

Fold right sides together, stitch ⅜in (9mm) from edge

Perfect curved seams
When sewing a curved seam, you will find that you get less drag and distortion on the seam if you start at the halfway point and stitch each side separately.

Flat-fell seam: A very strong, neat seam with a decorative finish. With wrong sides of fabric together, stitch on the seam line. Press the seam to one side. Trim inner seam allowance to $\frac{1}{8}$in (3mm). Press under the edge of the outer seam $\frac{1}{4}$in (6mm). Stitch this folded edge to the fabric.

Bias strips: First, find the bias of the fabric. Fold over a corner of the fabric to meet the cut edge, the diagonal fold is the bias of the fabric. Cut through this fold. Use a ruler and tailors' chalk to measure strips of the desired width from the diagonally-cut edge.

Pin, baste and stitch strips together along the straight grain ends.

Place the cord centrally to the wrong side of the fabric and fold the strip around the cord. Baste closely against the cord. With a piping foot on the sewing machine, stitch down the strip close beside the cord.

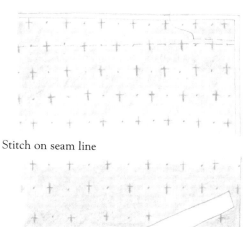

Stitch on seam line

Trim inner seam allowance

Stitch the folded edge down

Fold over a corner to find the bias

Measure strips from the diagonal cut edge

FINISHING TOUCHES

Piping: Piping is a strip of bias-cut fabric, folded and set into a seam for a decorative finish. For a harder-wearing finish, such as on cushions, the piping covers cord.

Piping cord comes in several thicknesses for different applications. To estimate the width of the covering fabric measure around the cord and then add 1$\frac{1}{4}$in (15mm).

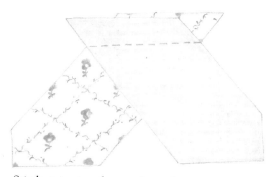

Stitch strips together on the ends

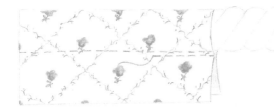

Stitch the fabric around the cord

Stitch the covered cord between the fabric layers

Inserting piping: Baste the prepared piping between two fabric layers, matching raw edges. Stitch on the seam line.

Joining piping: Start stitching $\frac{3}{8}$in (9mm) from the end. When you come to the other end trim the cord to meet the first cord. Trim the fabric covering back to $\frac{1}{2}$in (12mm). Butt the cords, dab a touch of fabric adhesive to the ends so that they stick together. Fold under the trimmed fabric edge $\frac{1}{4}$in (6mm). Wrap over the starting end of the piping. Continue stitching.

Frills
Single frill: Decide on the finished width of the frill and add $\frac{1}{2}$in (12mm) for a doubled hem and $\frac{5}{8}$in (15mm) for the seam allowance. To estimate the length, measure along the place to be frilled and double the measurement. (If the fabric is very thick, only allow one and a half times the measurement.) Turn a double $\frac{1}{4}$in (6mm) hem along the bottom edge. Press and machine stitch.

Work 2 rows of gathering stitches along the top edge either side of the seamline. (If the frill is very long, divide the frill into equal sections and gather each section in turn.) Pull the gathers up evenly to fit the main fabric. Pin then baste the frill to the main fabric, working across the gathering stitches to hold the frill in place. Stitch the frill in place. Remove basting threads. If the ends need to be neatened, work a double hem to match the bottom hem before gathering.

When making up a continuous frill, such as for a cushion, pin and stitch the frill strip short ends together into a ring before gathering.

Turn and stitch a double hem on a single frill

Work 2 rows of gathering along the top edge

For a continuous frill, stitch short ends together

Clever ways with ribbon
Polyester satin ribbon can be used for piping a seam. Fold 1in (2.5cm)-wide ribbon along the length, wrong sides facing. Pin and baste to the right side of fabric, matching the ribbon edges with the fabric raw edges. Place the second piece of fabric on top and stitch a $\frac{3}{8}$in (9mm) seam in the usual way.

Double frill: For a double frill, you need twice the required width and twice the seam allowance. Fold the strip lengthwise, wrong sides facing, and baste the raw edges

Baste and gather both layers together

Sewing tip

When instructions indicate that the seam allowance is to be added, first refold the fabric, right sides facing. Pin out the pattern. Draw around the outline of the pattern pieces using pencil or dressmaker's chalk pencil. (Add all marks etc.) Cut out ⅜in (9mm) from the pattern edge. Unpin the pattern. Baste the fabric pieces together, and stitch along the chalked line. This method enables you to achieve accurate stitching and perfect, straight seams.

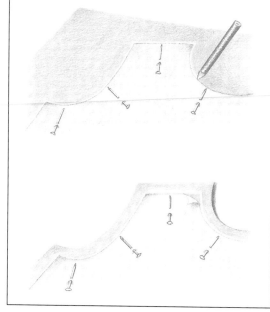

together. Then gather and apply the frill as for the single frill, working both layers together. If you need to neaten the ends, fold the frill ends right sides facing and stitch across the ends. Trim the seam allowance and turn the frill right side out. Then gather and apply as for the single frill.

Binding edges

Bias binding is a neat way of finishing a raw edge as well as adding a touch of color or pattern. Bias binding can be purchased ready-made in plain colored or patterned cotton or in acetate satin. If you wish to make your own bias binding, cut bias strips (see page 282). Press the sides of the strips to the center by one quarter.

To bind the edge of a piece of fabric, unfold one edge of the binding and lay against the fabric with right sides facing. The crease of the fold lies along the seamline. Pin, baste and stitch in the crease. Trim the fabric edge a little and fold the binding over the edge to the wrong side. Baste, then slipstitch in place, working over the previous stitches.

If the binding is to be topstitched, work the first stage of application in the same way. Bring the binding over the raw edge then baste and machine-stitch in place.

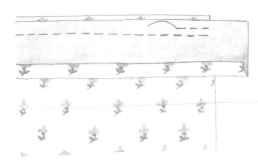

Open the binding and baste, then stitch, along the fold line

Fold the binding to the wrong side and slipstitch in place

Mitered corners

Mitering a turned-in edge: On a single hem, press under ¼in (6mm). Turn up the hem to the required length and press. Unfold and turn in the corner diagonally so that the diagonal fold meets the hem fold and press. Trim off the corner, leaving ¼in (6mm). Refold the hem over the trimmed corner.

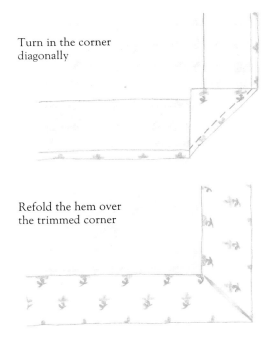

Turn in the corner diagonally

Refold the hem over the trimmed corner

Stitch the binding diagonally, trim off excess

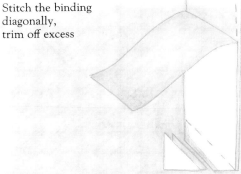

Stitch around the outside edge

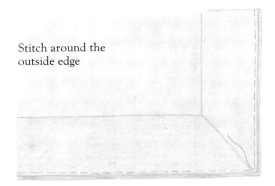

Stitch around the inside edge

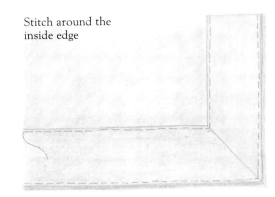

Mitering a flat trimming: Place the trim against the fabric edge; pin and stitch in place up to the corner and fasten. Fold the trimming back on itself, with the fold matching the next edge; pin firmly. Turn down the trimming along the next edge, pressing the diagonal fold that forms across the corner. Lift the trimming and stitch across the diagonal crease. Trim off excess and replace trimming. Continue stitching along the next edge. When all the corners have been mitered in the same way, stitch around the trimming along the inside edge.

Miter binding: Unfold the edge of the binding and place against the edge, as explained before. Pin and stitch in the crease of the binding up to the seam line of the next edge, fasten threads securely. Fold the binding diagonally away from the fabric, aligning the binding edge with the edge of the next side. Pin and stitch again, beginning the stitching from the seamline. Take the binding over the raw edge to the opposite side, folding the excess fabric into a neat miter. On the wrong side, tuck under the excess binding to form a neat miter as well. Pin and slipstitch the remaining folded edge of binding in place, stitching across the miter on each side, only when the binding is wide.

285

Index